ELIE KEDOURIE CBE, FBA 1926–1992

T0352800

Of Related Interest

Democracy and Arab Political Culture
edited by Elie Kedourie

*Afghani and 'Abduh: An Essay on Religious Unbelief and Political
Activism in Modern Islam*
by Elie Kedourie

Arab Political Memoirs and Other Studies
by Elie Kedourie

Towards A Modern Iran: Studies in Thought, Politics and Society
edited by Elie Kedourie and Sylvia G. Haim

The Chatham House Version and Other Middle Eastern Studies
by Elie Kedourie

*The Middle Eastern Economy: Studies in Economics and
Economic History*
edited by Elie Kedourie

Modern Egypt: Studies in Politics and Society
edited by Elie Kedourie and Sylvia G. Haim

Nationalism in Asia and Africa
edited by Elie Kedourie

Palestine and Israel in the 19th and 20th Centuries
edited by Elie Kedourie and Sylvia G. Haim

Zionism and Arabism in Palestine and Israel
edited by Elie Kedourie and Sylvia G. Haim

ELIE KEDOURIE CBE, FBA 1926–1992

History Philosophy, Politics

Edited by

SYLVIA KEDOURIE

FRANK CASS
LONDON • PORTLAND, OR

First published in 1998 in Great Britain by
FRANK CASS PUBLISHERS
Newbury House, 900 Eastern Avenue
London, IG2 7HH

and in the United States of America by
FRANK CASS PUBLISHERS
c/o ISBS, 5804 N.E. Hassalo Street
Portland, Oregon 97213-3644

Copyright © 1998 Frank Cass Publishers

Website http://www.frankcass.com

British Library Cataloguing in Publication Data

Elie Kedourie, CBE, FBA 1926–1992 : history, philosophy,
politics
   1. Kedourie, Elie 2. Middle East – Politics and government
I. Kedourie, Sylvia
320.9'56

ISBN 0-7146-4862-0 (cloth)
ISBN 0-7146-4419-6 (paper)

Library of Congress Cataloging-in-Publication Data

Elie Kedourie CBE, FBA, 1926–1992 : history, philosophy, politics /
edited by Sylvia Kedourie.
   p. cm.
   Includes bibliographical references.
   ISBN 0-7146-4862-0 (cloth). – ISBN 0-7146-4419-6 (paper)
   1. Kedourie, Elie. 2. Jews–England–London–Biography.
   3. Historians–Middle East–Biography. I. Kedourie, Sylvia.
DS135.E6K43   1997
956'.007'202 – dc21   97–40848
                                                          CIP

This group of studies first appeared as a supplement to
Middle Eastern Studies, Vol.33, No.4, October 1997,
'Elie Kedourie CBE, FBA 1926–1992: History, Philosophy, Politics'.

Elie Kedourie
1926–1992

Contents

Publisher's Note

I am particularly pleased to have this opportunity to write a short note to this well-deserved tribute volume to Elie Kedourie.

Middle Eastern Studies was the first scholarly journal published by Frank Cass. Elie Kedourie suggested the idea to me in July 1964 after the publisher who had commissioned him to produce the journal had decided against the project. We were very fortunate that *Middle Eastern Studies* was our first journal, because from the outset we benefited from Elie Kedourie's fine editing, impeccable scholarly standards and vision in publishing material by authors whose views he did not always share in a field then beset by extreme views. *Middle Eastern Studies* became, and remains, preeminent in its field.

In 1984, at a private reception held, ironically, at Chatham House to mark the twentieth anniversary of the journal, Elie pronounced himself delighted at the number of scholars and luminaries in the field who had had their first or very early work published in *Middle Eastern Studies*. To mark the thirtieth anniversary, in 1994, there was a celebration at the British Academy to launch the journal's thirty volume index – itself a veritable who's who of Middle Eastern erudition. Each occasion allowed us to reflect upon the journal's importance to scholarship.

From the very first issues, Sylvia G. Haim (Kedourie), herself a noted scholar, took on the onerous task of associate editor of the journal, and her publishing partnership with Elie Kedourie continued until his untimely death in 1992. The journal is most fortunate to have continued since 1992 under the distinguished editorship of Sylvia Kedourie.

In October, Frank Cass will celebrate forty years in publishing and during that time the company has launched sixty other scholarly journals, all of which have profited from the high ideals and standards imposed by Elie Kedourie on our first journal. We have also benefited from the constant support, advice and helpful publishing ideas offered by Elie and Sylvia Kedourie throughout this period. During these years the publishing friendship with Elie and Sylvia Kedourie has blossomed. It is an association of which I am immensely proud and will always cherish.

FRANK CASS
August 1997

Foreword

As this is the fifth anniversary of the passing of Elie Kedourie, the Founder and, until his death, the Editor of *Middle Eastern Studies* – a journal which, in the words of Frank Cass, served as a model for all subsequent journals published by him – this volume is offered as a tribute and a memorial to him. It is however not a biography but a commemoration. As an historian of the Middle East and Professor of Politics at the London School of Economics and Political Science (LSE), Elie Kedourie dealt with two major disciplines, and I hope that the various contributions to this volume will help to illumine his work and to give some idea of his personality.

Most contributors have remarked about Elie's reserve. I take this opportunity to include two pieces of his which have remained unpublished and which reveal a lot of the man. The first is the text of a short address he gave to a small group of colleagues who entertained him to dinner at his retirement from the LSE. In it he recounts the accidents of fate that brought him to the LSE as well as his first encounter with politics on the ground. The second is an article based on a public lecture which he gave at Brandeis University in the spring of 1991 and which encapsulates his antecedence of two and a half millennia.

Elie is widely linked with Michael Oakeshott. I therefore include the few words he said at the Memorial meeting for Michael Oakeshott at the LSE in 1991 where he tells of his own discovery of Oakeshott and subsequent meeting with him. Although not intended for publication, I gave this short piece – a five-minute talk which he was allocated for the memorial – to Jesse Norman, who published it in *The Achievement of Michael Oakeshott* (Duckworth, 1993).

Kamal Salibi's 'Tribute', first published in *Middle Eastern Studies: A Thirty Volume Index 1964–1994*, is reprinted here and heads a list of varied contributions. Michael Leifer, as the Pro-Director of LSE, was the first speaker at the Memorial Meeting for Elie on 20 January 1993. His address, printed here, is followed by the addresses of Kenneth Minogue, Regina Allen, David Pryce-Jones and Itamar Rabinovich. Peter Roberts, who also spoke, has sent in an expanded version of his address. P. J. Vatikiotis's 'Overview' brings to the fore not only Elie's eminence in scholarship but also the sort of attacks – so often anonymous – which he had to face right through his academic career.

Noel's O'Sullivan's 'Memoir' recreates his time as a graduate student at the LSE, and brings in that element of irreverence which is essential for drawing Elie's true picture. Michael Sutton and Liora Lukitz are two other scholars who recount their response to his teaching and guidance. Andrew Mango, Oliver Letwin (whose essay was first given as a Radio Three talk), Louise Greenberg and Joseph Shattan, all add detail which helps to flesh out his profile. Paschalis Kitromilides expresses an intellectual debt.

The essay by Alain Silvera, a much shorter version of which appeared in *The Times Literary Supplement* of 28 September 1995, answers in some measure Alan Beattie's remark about the difficulty of extracting Elie's general or 'real' views on the central issues recurring in his writings. Alan Beattie, whose essay was commissioned by the British Academy and part of which was published in the *Proceedings of the Academy, No. 87*, was a close colleague in the Government Department at LSE. His insight rounds off this collection.

Contributors to this volume worked independently of one another and did not have access to what each was writing. Consequently there is bound to be overlapping of material, but I decided to leave each essay as written in order not to break the flow of the argument. Except for correcting slight factual errors, I have not altered anything even when I was not totally in agreement with the author's interpretation.

I would like to express my thanks to all the contributors to this volume; thanks are also due to Frank Cass who has been so encouraging, and to Jonathan Manley who handles the work of *Middle Eastern Studies* so quietly and so efficiently. But most of all I would like to acknowledge the friendship of Peter and Diana Roberts, and to offer special thanks to Peter for his unstinting willingness to discuss, comment and correct.

SYLVIA KEDOURIE
April 1997

Elie Kedourie: A Tribute

KAMAL SALIBI

My friendship with the Kedouries dates back to 1950, Elie and Sylvia were then newly married, living in a small flat in Swiss Cottage. Elie, already working on his doctoral thesis at St Antony's College, Oxford; Sylvia, like myself, in her first year as a postgraduate Middle Eastern history student at the School of Oriental and African Studies, in the University of London. So Sylvia, naturally, was the first of them whom I met. Both of us were studying under Bernard Lewis: I, trying to discover why the Maronite Christians of the Lebanon, at different periods, conceived of their medieval history the way they did; Sylvia, seeking to determine the ways and means by which the nineteenth century European notions of liberalism and nationalism had first found their way to the Arab world. And so the friendship between us began and we discovered the extent to which our minds met on so many matters.

At Oxford, Elie, at the time, was doing something very daring. He was set on writing a critical appraisal of the standard British version of how the modern Arab world came to be – what he was later to term the 'Chatham House Version'. In his opinion, the English (meaning the British political establishment), having succeeded in destroying the Ottoman Empire, had brazenly proceeded to invent a national history for the system of Arab nation-states they themselves had artificially created on its ruins – a phoney history which had to be exposed for what it really was. I could not imagine Elie's examiners at Oxford easily passing a thesis questioning the competence and intellectual integrity of a British Arabist establishment of which they happened to be leading (if not *the* leading) representatives. And ultimately the thesis was not passed as presented. A number of modifications were required, which Elie refused to make because he thought differently. So he never received his Ph.D.

When I completed my studies in London and returned to Beirut in 1953, his relations with his examiners had already reached breaking point; he had also decided to leave Oxford and accept an offer to teach Political Science at the London School of Economics. The next time I returned to visit London, the Kedourie thesis the examiners had referred had just been published in book form, under the title *England and the Middle East: The Destruction of the Ottoman Empire, 1914–1921* (1956); and even scholars who disagreed with what the book had to say were finding it difficult to explain why they disagreed. Many of them could only join in acclaiming it a masterpiece on its subject, albeit a 'naughty' or 'mischievous' one (as I then heard it said). In passing his final verdict on British policy in the Middle East, Elie attributed its ultimate failure to the fact that 'English statesmen allowed themselves to believe that to satisfy the lust for power of discontented and ambitious men [with reference to the nationalists in Syria and Iraq] was virtuous and excellent.' The context in which he said this is worth quoting:

> ... the ends and means of Powers bear very little looking into; but what redeems their operations and invests them with a measure of grace is the acknowledged responsibility to see that order, security and legality obtain in the countries where their sway is exercised ... English domination in the Middle East meant both an opportunity and a responsibility. That the opportunity was missed, and the responsibility shirked is perhaps not surprising, since whatever happiness or peace or security men enjoy seems the result more of providential good fortune than of prudent exertion.

The subject we invariably came around to discuss, every time Elie and I got together, was nationalism in general, and nationalism in the Middle East. From our first discussion, Elie made it clear to me that he considered nationalism, as all political ideology, to be not only intrinsically inane but also pernicious, because it could so easily serve as a guise for naked ambition. I tended to agree, give or take the few reservations on points of detail which kept our discussions alive. Then came the day when I finally saw Elie's ideas on nationalism in print, beautifully articulated in a book bearing that title (*Nationalism*, first published in 1960). He wrote as plainly and directly as he spoke:

> Nationalism is a doctrine invented in Europe at the beginning of the nineteenth century ... Not the least triumph of this doctrine is that [its] propositions have become accepted as self-evident ... [and] firmly naturalized in the political rhetoric of the West which has taken over for the use of the whole world ...
>
> The attempts to refashion ... the world on national lines has not led to greater peace and stability. On the contrary, it has created new conflicts, exacerbated tensions, and brought catastrophe to numberless people innocent of all politics. The history of Europe since 1919, in particular, has shown the disastrous possibilities inherent in nationalism. In the mixed area of Central and Eastern Europe, and the Balkans, empires disappeared ... Whether these empires were doomed anyway, or whether it would have been possible to preserve them is mere speculation. What can be said with

certainty is that the nation-states who inherited the position of the empires were not an improvement. They did not minister to political freedom, they did not increase prosperity, and their existence was not conductive to peace; in fact, the national question which their setting up, it was hoped, would solve, became, on the contrary, more bitter and envenomed ... What may be said of Europe can with equal justice be said of the Middle East, or of South-East Asia, wherever the pressure of circumstances or the improvidence of rulers or their failure of nerve made possible the triumph of nationalist programmes.

In *England and the Middle East*, as in *Nationalism* and all his subsequent writings, Elie expressed himself plainly and with consistence and sincerity. In writing, as in conversation, he never minced words or beat about the bush; and if he was intolerant or unforgiving of anyone, it was of scholars who, behaving as politicians, did not express themselves in a straightforward manner, or whom he suspected of being deliberately devious. He was one person, it seemed to me, who conceived of scholarship as a public trust: a responsibility demanding complete and honest delivery, no matter the reaction such delivery may elicit. And that was what I – and I believe most of those who knew Elie well – admired in him most. The standards he maintained in his own scholarship, and expected from the scholarship of others, were exacting because to him things mattered, as they did not always matter to others.

My favourite among Elie's writings is his book on *Afghani and 'Abduh* (1966): the acknowledged vanguards, in the late nineteenth century and early twentieth, of Islamic modernism (as opposed to Islamic fundamentalism). Before Elie presented me with a copy of this book, someone had described it to me as a 'slender book of hate'. Generations of Arabs and Arabists, Muslims and Islamicists had been taught to take Afghani and 'Abduh seriously. Since my undergraduate days, however, I had always had the feeling that the two men had perhaps been praised far beyond their true worth, as neither of them, it seemed to me, had really grappled with the subject in his reformist thinking, or provided a perceptive critique of the subject. I tended to attribute this to their intellectual timidity; that both of them knew or had in mind more than they dared to say. Elie, however, provided a different explanation. Afghani and 'Abduh, he argued, were essentially agnostic modernists who said to their European friends, but not to their fellow Muslims, what they really thought. In recompense, 'the "Enlightened" modernists have been welcomed in the citadel of orthodoxy and welcomed as its most resourceful defenders'. He came to see that they were advocates of superficial reform which only served to undermine long-established religious tradition.

I was stopping in London on my way to the United States, in the spring of 1963, when Elie spoke to me for the first time of his decision to undertake the publication of a quarterly journal of Middle Eastern studies in association with a willing London publisher. Not the wisest of projects, I thought. For a learned journal to gain the required degree of academic recognition, it needed to be produced by a learned society, not by an individual, no matter the person's standing. There were, of course, exceptions; but was he sure the journal he proposed to produce would be one such exception? Wait and see. And I did not have to wait long before I saw. Elie Kedourie's *Middle Eastern Studies*, now in its fourth decade, had scarcely appeared before it was acclaimed as a leading periodical publication in the field, even by its editor's most determined critics.

If the standards Elie maintained in his scholarship and thinking were exacting, so were those he maintained in his friendship – a friendship all the more valued by those who enjoyed it because of the economy and good taste by which it was signalled. Elie was a person on whose constancy, generous forbearance and magnanimity of character, not to mention his quiet and gentle courtesy, one could always count. He was gracious and dignified ever since I first knew him; and a father figure he came to be in due course to his many students and admirers. I was privileged to have enjoyed his friendship for more than four decades. And it is a special honour for me to have been asked by Sylvia to write this tribute to his memory.

Michael Oakeshott: A Colleague's View

ELIE KEDOURIE

I became familiar with Michael Oakeshott's name while still an undergraduate at LSE. It was probably in 1949 that I first came upon his introduction to Hobbes's *Leviathan*, read it and re-read it. Here was a writer, it then seemed to me, who approached political thought in a profound and subtle way – who did not look upon it as a storehouse from which to draw arguments in favour of this or that political position, or as a compendium of slogans which have somehow accumulated down the ages. For the undergraduate reader the introduction opened up vistas of profundity and subtlety which challenged him to respond with a deepening and refining of his thought.

This text, however, remained a text – the glittering expression of a clearly exceptional mind. It stood as a monument calling upon you to comprehend its quality and power, but giving no clue, indeed providing no incentive, to discover what kind of man its author was.

It was during those same undergraduate years, 1949 and 1950, that I also came upon Oakeshott as editor of the *Cambridge Journal*. It was two articles published in there that made the man more accessible, that gave one the feeling that one could hold friendly converse, and perhaps tentatively explore possible affinities, with him. Curiously enough neither of the two articles was by Michael Oakeshott. One was by the economist S.R. Dennison and the other by C.H. Sisson. Dennison examined an attempt by an official working party (a title which I suppose indicated an aspiration to military despatch and efficiency) to establish how many nurses would be necessary two or three decades hence. Sisson explored, Conrad-like, the ambiguous world in which civil servants and politicians conducted their equivocal transactions. The textbooks at our disposal had, by contrast, assured us that economists and other social scientists could, with the utmost confidence, paint down to the smallest detail the lineaments of our future; and that the prime minister sat, *primus inter pares*, in the cabinet room, while secretaries, under-secretaries, assistant-secretaries and principals, like the members of an angelic hierarchy, transmitted, each in his turn, his wise and benevolent directions. Amid the intellectual dreariness of those post-war years, to discover two such articles in one periodical gave one a thrill of intellectual liberation – an intellectual liberation for providing which the editor of the *Cambridge Journal* I felt to be above all responsible.

Though I did not then know Oakeshott personally, in 1951 and 1952, while I was still a graduate student, I sent him two pieces which he accepted and published in the *Cambridge Journal*. The articles dealt with subjects with which he could not have been very familiar, but on the strength of what I sensed from the way he edited the *Journal* I felt that what I had to say might strike a responsive chord. And this is what I found when I came to know him as a colleague. His intellectual judgements were self-assured and acute. He found a way of going swiftly to the heart of the matter and seeing the essentials of an issue. It was this which until the end of his life gave an incomparable sparkle and charm to his mind, and which had the power to elicit in colleagues and friends during daily familiar intercourse an answering sparkle.

I became Michael's colleague in 1953, and it was my good fortune to remain one until his retirement. For most of these years he was the head of the Department of Government. The Department was a large one, and grew larger during his tenure. All those years he despatched its affairs with efficiency, economy and elegance. He did this with seeming effortlessness. So much so that, to me at any rate, it looked as though the Department ran itself.

When I retired my colleagues gave me a dinner at which I quoted a passage from Macaulay's *History*, which I would like to reproduce here. Speaking of the character of the English Parliament, Macaulay said:

> To think nothing of symmetry and much of convenience; never to remove an anomaly merely because it is an anomaly; never to innovate except when some grievance is felt; never to innovate except so far as to get rid of the grievance; never to lay down any proposition of wider extent than the particular case for which it is necessary to provide; these are the rules which have from the age of John to the age of Victoria generally guided the deliberations of our two hundred and fifty Parliaments.

In quoting this passage I had above all in mind the spirit of Michael's administration of the Department of Government.

If prudence, and the eschewing of sudden administrative jars and revolutions, were the hallmarks of Michael's long tenure as head of the Department, the case was quite otherwise with issues having to do with intellectual activity, the transmission of an intellectual tradition, and the criteria to be followed in determining the method and content of university teaching. Here, he was quick and decisive in establishing essentials and dismissing nonsense or flabbiness, however attractively or cunningly dressed up. I will end by illustrating this from his practice as a teacher.

In the nearly four decades of my life as a teacher at the School I have seen the academic board periodically seized with the desire to reform and improve the undergraduate degree, in response to some obscure but delusive urge to fashion a perfect, foolproof syllabus. One such convulsion gave Michael the opportunity to introduce his course on political thought, which became celebrated among the undergraduates. The course showed with what sureness of touch he married a commanding vision of the various styles of doing politics in the Western world, their vocabulary and idiom, with the requirements of an undergraduate audience, generally new to this kind of subject.

On another, later, occasion a fiat was handed down from Park Crescent, one of the first precursors of a deluge to come in succeeding years, that one-year graduate courses had to be instituted. The reasons were probably misconceived and banausic, and are now probably forgotten. Here too Michael seized the opportunity to establish a graduate course on the history of political thought. The course was genuinely a graduate course, in that it was not a simple extension of an undergraduate course but a philosophical inquiry into the organizing ideas of any possible history of political thought. For this course he composed a series of papers which were read at a Tuesday afternoon seminar which, for those who took part in it, was a landmark in the teaching week. He continued to take the leading part in the seminar until 1980, long after his official retirement, and the papers he composed for it are now accessible in the volume *On History*, published in 1983 and dedicated to the seminar.

Goethe said that reading Kant was like entering a room filled with light. To those who were able to enjoy the sunlit and well-ordered domain of Michael's mind, the fortunate experience will remain with them, always.

Retirement Dinner Address

ELIE KEDOURIE

This is my thirty-seventh year [June 1990] as a teacher in the Department of
Government, but my connection with the School is even older. It is 42 years
since I joined as an undergraduate. This is the better part of a lifetime, and
in chronological terms it is a very long time indeed. Film-makers
distinguish between filming 'real time' and 'imagined time'. In terms of
'imagined time' much of this long period is to me vividly present – as
though it were being lived here and now. There is the advertisement on the
back of the *New Statesman*, seen by chance in Baghdad, which invited
applications to sit for an entrance examination to LSE. There is my first day
at the LSE when, in a milling crowd in the Students' Union, a fellow
student, now a Tory knight, made himself known to me and invited me to
accompany him to a meeting – about what was not specified – which was
taking place in a room on what is now the 3rd floor, near the Robinson
Room. This turned out to be a recruitment meeting for the Communist
Society. Membership forms were handed round and it was explained that,
when filled, the forms would go to King Street. This was my first contact
with politics at LSE.

This, however, was not my very first acquaintance with politics, or with
the kind of politics agitated in the meeting to which I had been led. Having
grown up in what Michael Oakeshott has called an 'imitation state', I had a
sense, quite powerful even though still not very articulate, of the
degradation and thuggishness of politics in a state of this kind. As to
communism in particular, I knew that some of my school friends belonged
to the (secret and illegal) Iraqi Communist Party. What this exactly entailed
I was not very clear. A memory, however, remains with me of an episode in
my penultimate year at school. It was probably in an English lesson. I
cannot remember what the subject or the question was, but I still see the tall,
gangling schoolboy standing up at his desk and telling our master with the
self-assured smile of someone imparting a potent revelation, that freedom is
the recognition of necessity. I suppose he must have got this from some
penny dreadful by some Palme Dutt or other. The impression left on me was
that here was a nasty potion, Marxism, which those who had the means or
the power to do so derived great pleasure from administering. For this
hectoral doctrine I felt an aversion, perhaps derived from *Darkness at Noon*

which I must have read about then. This my kindly guide could not, however, know.

My second encounter with politics at LSE happened, also by chance, a few months later in February 1948, when I put my head into the Old Theatre and found it absolutely packed with students. It was a Students' Union meeting called to discuss the recent Communist take-over in Prague, and there on the rostrum was an emissary of the Czech Embassy explaining with a salesman's fluency why the Communists simply had to take over. I do not know whether the man is still alive, but in 1968 he came back as a refugee from Communism and got a university post teaching literature and literary criticism.

These were episodes in an education in politics. They happened by chance. Both as students and teachers we have of course to conform to syllabuses and to a degree structure. This is undoubtedly necessary, but what has struck me all these years is the chancy character of what makes for education – when a spark is struck or when it fails to be struck – when, as Plato puts it in the Seventh Letter, a light flashes forth and a fire is kindled.

Such occasions are present and vivid to me now, as for instance, a short course of lectures on French constitutions from 1790 to 1946 which was given by Bill Pickles, and which impressed on me the extreme fragility of the French political order; or another short course of lectures by Morris-Jones on the Government of India under the East India Company and under the Crown – which gave me an idea of the great difficulty of marrying constitutional government with a tradition of oriental despotism; or again a casual conversation with Martin Wight, the first time I met him by pure chance, when he put before me a vision of European history as one in which – from Charlemagne to Hitler – various rulers are seen to succumb to the temptation of achieving an imperial dominion replicating that of Rome.

These were incidents – formative incidents – in the intellectual life of an undergraduate. Bill, Morris, Martin Wight, or indeed I myself, could not have had at the time the slightest inkling that these would be elements forming in their listener an individual and distinctive outlook on politics. I am sure that this goes on all the time – this mysterious alchemy between teacher and taught, in intercourse among colleagues, which cannot be codified – and the outcome of which is an education.

In the words of probably the most ancient prayer of the Synagogue, recited daily for over two thousand years, we call down a blessing 'upon our masters, upon their disciples and upon the disciples of their disciples'.

When I joined the Department in 1953, Michael Oakeshott was its head and was to remain so for many years afterwards. He conducted its business with elegant economy, writing his letters and memoranda with his own hand. No doubt the mass of predominantly superfluous business which now oppresses conveners had not then been heard of, nor did we know that, lurking in the wings were the commissars with their numbers games and their planning itch. I was myself convener from 1975 to 1978 and I remember my great astonishment when someone asked me what the Department's policy or plan was!

There is a passage in Macaulay's *History* in which he describes the character of the English parliament. He says:

> To think nothing of symmetry and much of convenience; never to remove an anomaly merely because it is an anomaly; never to innovate except when some grievance is felt; never to innovate except so far as to get rid of the grievance; never to lay down any proposition of wider extent than the particular case for which it is necessary to provide; these are the rules which have from the age of John to the age of Victoria generally guided the deliberations of our two hundred and fifty Parliaments.

I cannot say that Macaulay is right in his judgement of Parliament – but think his words describe perfectly the ethos of the Department's (and of the School's) administration as it fortunately was during much of the time that I served it.

I have, indeed, been very fortunate in belonging to such a department and in the colleagues and friends who individually and collectively made possible so satisfying and so happy a career.

I raise my glass to the Department and to you all, my friends and colleagues.

The Jews of Babylon and Baghdad

ELIE KEDOURIE

The Jews of Baghdad today number perhaps a hundred and fifty, perhaps two hundred. They are a tiny remnant of a once large, flourishing and influential community. This community descended in a continuous, uninterrupted line (as the records show) from those Jews who, in 597 BCE, came to Babylon with Yehoiakin, King of Judah, deported thither by Nebuchadnezzar, King of Babylon (and of much else). We are told in the Book of Kings that Nebuchadnezzar

> carried away all Jerusalem, and all the princes, and all the mighty men of valour, even ten thousand captives, and all the craftsmen and smiths

and that

> none remained save the poorest sort of the people of the land

> (II Kings, 24:14)

The deportation came about by reason of the rivalry between the two Great Powers of the period, Babylon and Egypt, and the failure of the Kings of Judah to steer a prudent course between them. The deportation, undoubtedly a harsh measure, did not however mean that those deported were deprived of livelihood, or reduced to slavery, or forbidden to practise their religion, or to consort with one another. Rather, as a Babylonian inscription records, the deportees were assigned dwelling-places 'in the most convenient districts of Babylon' (Elias Bickerman, *From Ezra to the Last of the Maccabees*, 1962, p.6), where they established settlements and cultivated the land. It is interesting and significant that the narrative of the Second Book of Kings concludes by describing how in the thirty-seventh year of Yehoiakin's captivity (he was twenty-six years of age when taken captive), Nebuchadnezzar's successor, Evil-Merodakh,

> did lift up the head of Yehoiakin King of Judah out of prison, and he spoke kindly to him, and set his throne above the throne of the kings that were with him in Babylon, and changed his prison garments, and he did eat bread continually before him all the days of his life. And his allowance was a continual allowance given him of the King, a daily rate for every day, all the days of his life.   (II Kings, 25:27–30)

What is beyond doubt is that these deportees did establish a Jewish society

which became rooted in the land of their exile, thus following the
exhortation of the Prophet Jeremiah who, as is well known, was bitterly
opposed to the foreign policies of the kings of Judah, an opposition for
which he paid heavily, even perhaps with his own life. In the interval
between the deportation of Yehoiakin in 597 and Nebuchadnezzar's second
expedition in 586 which devastated Jerusalem and destroyed the Temple,
Jeremiah advised the exiles to

> Build ye houses and dwell in them; and plant gardens, and eat the
> fruits of them; take ye wives, and beget sons and daughters; and take
> wives for your sons, and give your daughters to husbands, that they
> may bear sons and daughters; that ye may be increased there and not
> diminished. And seek the peace of the city whither I have caused you
> to be carried away captives, and pray unto the Lord for it; for in the
> peace thereof shall ye have peace.   (Jeremiah, 29:5–7)

We may say that for two and a half millennia, through numberless chances
and changes, in the midst of many vicissitudes, the descendants of the
Babylonian Captivity endeavoured, generally with success, and sometimes
with quite brilliant results, to conduct their affairs in the spirit of Jeremiah's
advice.

This record, very long and without interruption, may serve to illustrate
the philosophy of Jewish history associated with the name of Simon
Rawidowicz. This philosophy of history offered an organizing idea which
seeks to make sense of the very long and varied Jewish experience – an
experience marked by a strikingly distinct and strongly-marked identity.
Going against the fashionable and very powerful modern current,
Rawidowicz likened the historical experience of the Jews to an ellipse
which has two foci. One of them is the land of Israel and the other the
Diaspora. The distinctiveness of Rawidowicz's position is that he held these
two foci to be a permanent characteristic of Jewish history. He held that the
Diaspora is not a temporary phase, preparatory to some future ingathering
of the exiles, thus destined to evanescence, and deriving its significance
from that which is inevitably destined to supersede it. Unfashionable as this
vision of Jewish history now is, yet reflection must lead us to conclude that
only this organizing idea can make sense of Jewish experience as we know
it from its records. For Rawidowicz, the symbol of the Diaspora as one of
the permanent poles of Jewish life is Babylon.

The experience of Babylonian Jewry over many centuries, as well as
what they themselves made of this experience, shows how appropriately
Rawidowicz chose it to symbolize one of the two poles of Jewish history.
There are, as is well known, lists of the Babylonian Exilarchs extending
from 140 CE under the Parthians, to the middle of the thirteenth century,

after which they are lost to view. There are also lists of *geonim* who headed the *yeshivoth* at Sura and Pumbeditha and at Baghdad, which begin in 589 CE and end in 1288. There is, above all, the redaction of the Babylonian Talmud which is held to have taken place over a period extending from the first half of the fourth century CE to the end of the fifth century. All these developments thus come considerably later than the first settlement of the deportees in Babylon, but it cannot be imagined that they suddenly sprang up fully formed. This evidence argues, on the contrary, that during the centuries preceding the first recorded Exilarch, the first recorded *gaon* and the beginnings of the redaction of the Talmud, the Jews of Babylon must have enjoyed a strong and flourishing commercial life, and must have evolved a vigorous and original intellectual tradition.

Nor are we reduced to conjecture. Long before the succession of Exilarchs and *geonim* as we know it from the surviving evidence, we have the record of the activities of Ezra the Scribe and of Nehemiah. In 539 BCE Cyrus, the king of Persia, conquered Babylon and it was his successor Artaxerxes, the second of that name (as the authorities now argue), who issued a decree at the end of the fifth century BCE, empowering Ezra to proceed to Jerusalem. As we see from the text of the decree recorded in chapter 7 of Ezra, Ezra went there as an imperial commissioner, 'sent of the king, and of his seven counsellors, to enquire concerning Judah and Jerusalem, according to the law of thy God which is in thine hand'. Ezra was to take with him the treasures of the Temple looted by Nebuchadnezzar; he was to be accompanied by all the people of Israel, his priests and Levites 'which are minded of their free will to go up to Jerusalem'. Ezra was given the power to restore the worship and sacrifices of the Temple, and to appoint magistrates and judges 'who know the laws of thy God'; the decree also enjoined that 'whosoever will not do the law of thy God, and the law of the King, let judgment be executed speedily upon him, whether it be unto death, or to banishment, or to confiscation of goods, or to imprisonment' (Ezra, 7:13–2).

The other chief figure who played a most prominent part in these transactions was an important official at the court of Artaxerxes, Nehemiah. As we learn from his own account, when on one occasion he, as cup-bearer, served wine to Artaxerxes, the king remarked on his sad countenance. With trepidation Nehemiah said: 'Why should not my countenance be sad, when the city, the place of my fathers' sepulchres, lieth waste, and the gates thereof are consumed with fire?' Nehemiah then begged for permission to be sent to Jerusalem in order to rebuild it. Artaxerxes gave his permission, and Nehemiah served as the governor of Judah and Jerusalem for twelve years (Nehemiah, 2:1, 8; and 5:14).

There are many arresting features about this story. In the first place, almost two centuries had elapsed between the arrival of the deportees in

Babylon and the despatch of Ezra and Nehemiah to Jerusalem, armed with imperial authority, to restore the Temple and re-establish Judah as an entity on its own, albeit one subordinate to the Persian Empire. Here, then, is evidence that the Jews of Babylon had not only flourished, but had also influential and powerful representatives at the Persian court. It was from this disaspora, by now seemingly well rooted in Babylon, that the impulse came to restore the Temple and the City. We read in *Ezra* that he was accompanied only by those who were minded to leave Babylon for Jerusalem. The inference must be that those who decided to stay constituted the larger part.

Ezra and Nehemiah went to Jerusalem armed with imperial powers, in order to see to it that the laws of Judaism would be followed. We may thus say that it was in the benign shadow of the Persian Empire, extending from the Indus to Ethiopia, that Jewish communities and Judaism in Babylon and many other regions were able to subsist and to flourish. In this sense, therefore, Babylon became the centre of a Jewry dispersed throughout the Empire, yet held together by the practices and the teachings of Judaism and by attachment to Jerusalem, the city, in Nehemiah's words, of their fathers' sepulchres. We may even go further, and declare with Elias Bickerman that the Dispersion saved Judaism 'from physical extirpation and spiritual inbreeding' (op. cit., p.3).

As noted, Jeremiah enjoined the Jews of Babylon to pray for its peace, 'for in the peace thereof shall ye have peace'. He had another piece of advice to give them. God has declared, he told them, that it was He who gave the King of Babylon, his 'servant', all the lands over which Nebuchadnezzar has ruled,

> Therefore hearken not yet to your prophets nor to your diviners, nor to your dreamers, nor to your enchanters, nor to your sorcerers, which speak unto you, saying, ye shall not serve the King of Babylon, for they prophesy a lie unto you.   (Jeremiah, 27:5, 9–10)

From 597 BCE to 1950 CE the Jews of Babylon seem to have heeded this injunction, indication enough of which is the sobriety which has always characterized the community in public affairs.

No one knows where Nehemiah is buried. As for Ezra, his sepulchre, as a very old tradition attests, lies there in Babylon, a little way to the north of Basra. The Jews of Baghdad kept his memory green from that day to this. Ezra's tomb, at Uzayr, was, until the disappearance of the community, the object of a yearly pilgrimage which took place between Passover and Shevuoth. Another sepulchre was also an object of veneration for the Jews of Baghdad, the tomb of Ezekiel whose prophetic call came to him in Babylon. The tomb is at Kifl near Hillah to the south of Baghdad, and it was again uninterruptedly the object of yearly pilgrimages. The names, Ezra and Heskel, are indeed favourites among the Jews of Baghdad. This veneration for two figures who belong to the very earliest period of the settlement in Babylon is not the product of an antiquarian fancy, fabricated, as so many have been, by modern writers intent on discovering pedigrees or roots in order to promote some nationalist movement or another. It constitutes an unbroken chain, unselfconsciously maintained over the centuries and the generations, by the descendants of those who came with Yehoiakin to Babylon.

THE DESCENDANTS

It is, of course, impossible to assert that the Jews of Baghdad in the middle of the twentieth century were exclusively the lineal descendants, in a biological sense, of those who came to Babylon with Yehoiakin. Over the centuries newcomers undoubtedly kept on arriving from various countries. What is striking, however, is that the origin of families who, to judge by their names, must have been Sephardi or European or Caucasian, or Persian, or Central Asian, was very quickly forgotten by themselves and by the community at large where, as regards customs, behaviour and language, they were exactly like everyone else. A case in point relates to the guardians of Ezekiel's sepulchre in the twentieth century. These were the Daniel family, who were perhaps one of the two or three most prominent families in Baghdad during the six or seven decades preceding the dissolution of the community.

The Daniels were considerable landowners in the region of Hillah, and hence in the area of Kifl. They seem to have come from the Caucasus, and the origin of their landed wealth, as was frequently the case in the Ottoman Empire prior to the administrative reforms of the mid-nineteenth century, lay in tax-farming. They must have been relative newcomers, though it is not known exactly when they settled in Baghdad. By the twentieth century, however, it would have occurred neither to themselves nor to others that their origin, even if it had been remembered, made them any different from their fellow-Baghdadi Jews. Presumably because they were the most prominent landowners in the area in which Kifl was situated, they became the guardians of Ezekiel's sepulchre, and Menahem Daniel, the head of the family who died in 1940, was buried in proximity to the sepulchre, as were earlier members of the family. Menahem's son, Ezra, a senator like his father, stood up in the Senate in 1950 to raise a solitary voice against the official oppression which, following the establishment of Israel in 1948, had risen to a crescendo. His speech was an elegy on a community which had maintained itself in the same spot for two and a half millennia. Ezra too, when he died shortly afterwards – leaving no descendants – was buried by the side of his ancestors in the shrine of the Prophet Ezekiel.

The homogeneity and the assimilative power of the Baghdad Jewish community is in striking contrast to the state of affairs elsewhere. Whether in Jerusalem, or in North America, or in Venice, Amsterdam or London, for example, Jews who had different origins were always aware of these differences, and strove to perpetuate their separate communities, traditions and synagogues. In Baghdad, by contrast, there was always one community and one *minhag*.

Under the imperial order established by the Persian kings and their successors, whether Parthians, Sassanids, Abbasids or Ottomans, Babylonian Jewry was able sometimes to flourish and generally to maintain itself. The political, religious and intellectual leaders of the community were for long a motive power for Jewry and Judaism, in token of which the *qaddish de-rabbanan* came to include verses praying for the Exilarch and the *geonim*. In the ninth century CE, the *gaon* of the *yeshiva* at Sura, in a responsum to the community of Qayrawan in Tunisia, gives us an idea of the status which these leaders claimed, and which they were accorded. He writes that when the traveller Eldad ha-Dani 'said that they pray for the scholars of Babylon and then for those in the Diaspora, they are right. For the major scholars and prophets were exiled to Babylon, and they established the *Torah* and founded the academy on the Euphrates under Yehoiakin, King of Judah, until this day, and they were the dynasty of wisdom and prophecy and the source of *Torah* for the entire people' (*Encyclopedia Judaica*, Vol.7, pp.317–18).

The feeling that the centre of the Jewish people was indeed now Babylon had already been strongly expressed in the Babylonian Talmud, where the famous *amora*, Yehuda bar Yehezqel, the founder of the *yeshiva* at Pumbeditha, who died at the end of the third century CE, declared that 'Whoever goes from Babylon to the Land of Israel violates a positive commandment,' and quoted in support of his contention the verse in *Jeremiah* (27:22) which says, 'They shall be carried to Babylon and there they shall be until I remember them, sayeth the Lord, and bring them up and restore them to this place.' It was also Rabbi Yehuda's judgement that 'Whoever lives in Babylon it is as if he lives in the Land of Israel' (Babylonian Talmud, *Ketubot* 110b–111a, discussed in Simon Rawidowicz, *Israel the Ever-Dying People*, pp.215–16).

In his very fine essay, 'Sanctity, Praise and Deprecation', Rawidowicz quotes (op. cit., p.224) a passage from the *Tanhuma Midrash* in which it is declared that Israel 'dwelled with their *Torah* in Babylon ... and neither *Edom* nor *Yavan* ruled over them or decreed persecution upon them'. The Jews of Babylon had indeed little part to play in the momentous events which shook the Jews and Judaism when Jerusalem fell under Seleucid domination, and when subsequently, during the second century BCE, a Hellenizing party sought to gain the upper hand in Jerusalem – an attempt which sparked Matatiyahu's revolt in 166. Neither did Babylon play any part in the complex intrigues and the treacherous manoeuverings for power within the Hasmonean dynasty, or between them, the neighbouring rulers and their Seleucid overlords. Edom succeeded Yavan with Pompey's conquest of Jerusalem in 63 BCE, and the Jews of Palestine came under Roman rule – a fateful event marking profoundly Jewish life to this very day. A century later came the clash with Rome, the destruction of Jewish autonomy in the Land of Israel which had subsisted in various guises since the time of Ezra and Nehemiah. The Jews of Babylon had little direct contact with any of these events, and no say at all in the Jewish policies which eventuated in the siege of Jerusalem by Titus, in the devastation of the city and the sack of the Temple.

Tanhuma seems to have taught in the second half of the fourth century CE, and he could not have suspected the disastrous extent of what was so shortly to transpire. Christianity having been adopted by Constantine, Jews and Judaism would be gratefully and inexorably frozen out of the body politic, to be attacked, humiliated and ferociously persecuted, in obedience to successive enactments by the Emperors. These laws had force throughout the Roman Empire, east and west. Also, because the authority of Justinian's *Corpus Juris* (codified and proclaimed in the sixth century) was accepted in Christian Europe, the systematic persecution practised by an Edom converted to Christianity, justified and encouraged by the Church, would persist for a great many centuries, long after the disappearance of Roman and Byzantine power. From this unremitting pressure, the restrictions, the humiliations, and the perpetual insecurity that went with it, the Jews of Babylon were generally free. From the Captivity onwards they lived under rulers to whom it never occurred to enforce religious uniformity on their subjects, or punish religious difference. More pertinently, they did not claim that the religion they professed made them the true Israel, and that therefore the very survival of Jews and Judaism was a standing, and an intolerable, offence.

On the contrary, the empires under whom the Jews of Babylon successively lived took it for granted that the communities subject to them would worship their own gods, and practise the rites peculiar to them. It is true that Islam – the encounter with which came fairly late in Jewish history – claimed that Muhammad was the seal of the Prophets, and that the refusal of Jews and Christians to recognize this was wilful blindness. But Islam did not nurse the same obsession with this refusal to recognize the truth of the new revelation, and above all Islam did not accuse the Jews of the ultimate crime of having killed the Founder of their religion.

In the course of time the idea of religious toleration arose in parts of Western Europe. It was the outcome of a deadlock between contending versions of Christianity. It did not, however, necessarily mean that individuals had full liberty to practise whatever religion they wished. In the German-speaking world after the Treaty of Westphalia it signified rather that the subject's religion had to follow that of the ruler. This religious toleration meant little or no change in the Jewish condition in Europe. In due course, the scepticism, not to say cynicism, induced by sectarian strife which had come to seem both excessive and meaningless, led to political secularization in Europe. The state now demanded that loyalty to it should supersede every other. In the case of the Jews this meant that they had to purchase admission into the secular polity by renouncing whatever elements of social and religious organization the state judged to be incompatible with the citizenship it was conferring upon them. Jews had to prove their full loyalty by doing away with whatever distinguished them from the majority of the citizens, in other words by 'assimilating'. To such a process there was obviously no limit. However much Jews 'assimilated', there was always yet another proof which might be demanded in order to ensure that they were indeed qualified to be full citizens. The absurd, but logical, outcome of such a state of affairs is Bruno Bauer's demand that unless Jews totally renounced Judaism they could not become part of the body politic. For Jews this was a precarious situation politically, and spiritually as well. The demand from the outside that Jews should 'assimilate' became internalized in very many European Jews and led to much discomfort and even anguish, and to grotesque and pitiful contortions, exemplified by the phenomenon of Jewish 'self-hate'. For the historical reasons on which I have touched, the Jews of Babylon mercifully never came under this kind of pressure, and remained immune to the spiritual disorder which it produced.

For the last twelve hundred years of their history the Jews of Babylon lived under Muslim rule, and some time during this period they came to be concentrated in the city of Baghdad, which the Abbasids built as their capital in the middle of the eighth century, and where the Exilarchs and the *geonim* came to reside. Henceforth Babylonian Jewry is synonymous with Baghdad Jewry. Aramaic-speaking as they had been, the Jews of Baghdad were very quickly able to adopt the Arabic of the new rulers as their mother tongue, and so it remained until the end. It has been suggested, notably by the late Haim Blanc, that the Arabic spoken by the Jews of Baghdad up to the present day preserves the pronunciation and the morphology of Arabic as it was in Abbasid times, while spoken Arabic of the Muslims contains a considerable admixture of rough Bedouin speech, acquired by contact with the tribes which, taking advantage of the weakness of the central government in Ottoman times, and even earlier, continuously infiltrated the towns and settled in their environs. Baghdad Jewish speech does indeed contain many words and expressions dating back to early Islamic times, just as it embodies the occasional reminiscence of extremely remote events in Islamic history.

In contemporary Baghdad Jewish speech there is an expression meant to describe someone's destructive action: it is said to be like *fani Khēbar*, the devastation which befell Khaybar. Even though hardly anyone using the idiom can have realized it, it refers to that oasis north of Medina in the Hijaz inhabited by Jewish tribes, which Muhammad attacked in his vendetta against the Banu Nazir, one of the four Jewish tribes of Medina with whom he fell out, and which in consequence took refuge in Khaybar where it owned property. The expression, transmitted over the generations from the seventh or eighth century to the twentieth and, so far as is known, not used by anyone else, exemplifies the historical continuity which the pilgrimages to the tombs of Ezekiel and Ezra in their different ways also illustrate.

The Arabic translation of the Pesah *haggada* dating, in part at any rate, most probably from Abbasid times, written in Judeo-Arabic and read, passage by passage, together with the original Hebrew and Aramaic, is also instructive. The Arabic not only manages to give accurately the meaning of the original text, and convey its rhetorical charge, but also does this in a flexible language where the difference between the written and the spoken – the spoken as it has subsisted to this day – is minimal. This is in great contrast to the gulf created in modern times between the two, as a result of misguided purism on the part of linguists and grammarians, who have laboured to imprison a living language in the stiff corset of minute and fussy rules and prohibitions.

The Jews of Babylon and of Baghdad were of course subject to the same ups and downs as the larger society among whom they dwelt. During these long centuries Mesopotamia and Baghdad went through many obscure, and sometimes dark, epochs. Following the Ottoman conquest in the sixteenth century, Baghdad and indeed the whole region became a backwater, politically and in point of wealth and civilization. Only in the second half of the nineteenth century did it begin to revive. Economic activity was greatly stimulated by traffic with British India, and particularly by the opening of the Suez Canal in 1869. In this activity the Jews of Baghdad undoubtedly had the primacy. Also, in 1885, the Alliance Israélite Universelle opened a boys' school in Baghdad. Other schools followed in Mosul, Hilla and Basra, and notably a girls' school which opened in Baghdad in 1895. Baghdad Jews, again, increasingly established connections in India, Burma, the Far East and Manchester, and these colonies never lost touch with the mother community.

All these developments worked together to increase steadily the exposure of the Jews of Baghdad to the civilization of the West, and to secularize their outlook on the world. It is very often said that such a process is detrimental to Judaism and to the cohesion of the Jewish community. This was undoubtedly very true of European Jews, and particularly those of Central and Eastern Europe. However, among the Jews of Baghdad, the phenomena which served in Europe to point to the disintegration of Judaism and the Jewish community were remarkably absent during the century preceding the departure of the community to the state of Israel. Conversion to Islam or inter-marriage were, apart from a tiny handful of cases, quite unknown. so was religious schism within the community, or the advocacy of a militant, secularist ideology with its depreciation of Judaism, also prominent features of European Jewries in modern times.

In explanation of this state of affairs, the late Emile Marmorstein, who was well acquainted with the community in the second half of the 1930s, used to speak of a sociological religion. By this he meant that the Judaism of the Baghdad Jews had ceased to be a matter of belief and observance, and had been reduced to a mere badge of group solidarity. No one will know if it would ultimately have come to this, but the fact remains that, until its disappearance, the community still maintained an extensive network of religious, educational and other institutions, and there is no evidence to show that they were then on the road to disintegration, or that the Baghdad Jews were abandoning loyalty to Judaism.

Marmorstein's view was predicated on the assumption that a Jewish response to Western civilization could be only one of two kinds: either resistance to it root-and-branch, or its full acceptance, this latter inevitably leading, sooner or later, to the utter emasculation of Judaism. These, however, are not necessarily the only possible outcomes. As Elias Bickerman had brilliantly shown, those against whom Matatiyahu started his rebellion had wished to assimilate the Torah to Hellenism. His successors in the Hasmonean House wished, by contrast, to incorporate Hellenic culture in the Torah. The Pharisees who made Judaism as we know it today were profoundly touched by Hellenism, in particular by the belief, 'the Platonic notion', writes Bickerman, 'that education could so transform the individual and the entire people that the nation would be capable of fulfilling the divine task set [for] it.' The Pharisees, again, contrary to the Sadducees, wished to supplement the Torah of Moses with the 'oral' law. 'This singular notion,' adds Bickerman, 'of setting traditional usage or *halakhah* alongside the written law is again Greek. It is the concept of the "unwritten law" which is preserved not on stone or paper but lives and moves in the actions of the people' (Bickerman, op. cit., pp.162–4). As I have said, there is no knowing what consequences exposure to the Western secular mind-set would eventually have had for the Jews of Baghdad, since the outcome of intellectual and cultural influences takes a very long time to work out, and its character is never a foregone conclusion. The little evidence that we have seems to show that the leading *rabbanim* of the latter half of the nineteenth century and the beginning of the twentieth, Hakham Abdullah Somekh (d.1889) and Hakham Yosef Hayyim (d.1906) inclined to think that accommodation with Western culture was the wisest way of dealing with the challenge.

The British occupation of Baghdad in 1917 heralded, though no one would have suspected it, the beginning of the last epoch of the Jews of Babylon in the country which had been theirs for two-and-a-half millennia. In 1917, and indeed until they left in 1950–51, the Jews constituted the largest group in a city inhabited by two other main groups, Sunnis and Shiis. Middle Eastern historical demography is inexact at best and extremely murky at worst. Many figures for the Jewish population of Baghdad are found in various sources in different centuries. It is said, for instance, that in the Persian Empire, Jews were a majority in Babylonia. No numbers or estimates are available for many centuries thereafter. Benjamin of Tudela gave some figures, and Benjamin II many centuries afterwards gave another set of figures. Other nineteenth-century travellers give yet other statistics incompatible with one another. The only figures possessed of any exactness are those indicating the numbers of people who were registered to go to Israel in 1950–51. They amounted to 120–130 thousand. Regardless of exact numbers, however, it is clear that whenever they make an appearance on the historical scene, the Jews are almost always seen to play a prominent part in the affairs of Baghdad.

The period after 1917 was no exception. Five years or so after this date, the British invented a new state to which they gave a mock-antique name, Iraq. Ten years after, this state was endowed with full sovereignty. The Jews were now citizens of a state where Shiis were a majority, Kurds a sizeable minority, but which was governed by a small Sunni Arab minority. The regime was headed by a king who was a foreigner, and its main pillars were upstarts of whom nobody had heard before. From the beginning the new Kingdom thus harboured the seeds of considerable violence – violence which, over the decades, became progressively more destructive.

In the three decades between the creation of Iraq and their exodus, stateless and deprived of their possessions, the Jews of Baghdad held a prominent position in the economy, and were engaged besides in the variety of occupations and professions, legal, scientific, artistic and administrative, called for by the needs of an increasingly sophisticated society. Yet it was apparent from the mid-1930s that their position was becoming more shaky. The government enjoyed little legitimacy. It was a government of Arab Sunnis intent on imposing themselves on a country the vast majority of which was neither Sunni nor Arab. To maintain themselves in power, and to guard against the intrigues and plots of rivals, the men in power, fearing any local initiative or communal autonomy, adopted increasingly brutal and oppressive centralizing policies. These men were also wedded to a pan-Arab policy. They looked upon Iraq as the Prussia or the Piedmont of the future all-Arab state. Pan-Arab politics and intrigues increasingly engaged their interest. From 1936 onwards, they endeavoured to act as the champions of the Palestine Arabs in their resistance to Zionism, and Palestine Arabs, many of them imported as school-teachers, did their best to influence the zeal of the official classes for their cause. The situation of the Jews of Baghdad in consequence steadily deteriorated.

I may illustrate the despondency which this lowering political climate induced by quoting from a letter written in the summer of 1942. I was then an adolescent schoolboy. A school-friend of mine had been having a correspondence with the well-known French writer, André Gide. He happened to show me a letter in which Gide, somewhat vapidly, exhorted him at all costs to remain hopeful. I had read some of Gide's writings from which I received the impression that he was the apostle not of hopefulness, but of disquietude. I thought his letter to my friend out of character with these writings and, more important, quite at variance with the state of the world as I was coming to know it. I therefore penned a letter to him, some passages of which have survived only because he proceeded to quote them in a lecture which he published, and of which he sent me a copy. In my letter I expressed astonishment at his readiness to preach hope. 'In these times of anguish and distress which have just begun,' I wrote, 'to accept to hope is to demean oneself.' On the contrary, I said, to be disquieted is the only attitude which I considered valid, and which would preserve our integrity. I added that it was a Jew who was writing to him. For an unknown reason, Gide did not include this detail in the passages which he included in his lecture. It was, however, a material detail, since without it the letter reads as though it is a mere expression of generalized cosmic anguish. Half a century has passed since this letter was written, and I cannot with any precision recall the exact reasons which led me to write as I did. It has to be remembered however that the previous summer the Jews of Baghdad had been the victim of a murderous assault on their lives, honour and possessions, following the collapse of an anti-British government, when the city was left without law and order, while British troops standing at the gates were forbidden from intervening by an infamous prohibition on the part of the British ambassador, Sir Kinahan Cornwallis. At any rate, there is no doubt in my mind that what I was seeing and sensing all around me gave their impetus to the strong feelings which found expression in my letter to Gide. (Extracts from letter in André Gide, *Souvenirs littéraires et problèmes actuels*, Beirut 1946.)

The crisis which had been brewing since the mid-1930s became manifest in all its ferocity in 1948. It took barely two years before successive bouts of increasingly severe official persecution, enforced with the administrative techniques of modern despotism, induced desperation and panic in the Jews of Baghdad. The assumptions on which Zionist doctrine had been erected, as well as the social and political pressures which made the doctrine persuasive and its programme plausible, were all quite unfamiliar to them. In 1950 their fear and panic led them to embrace a way out offered by Iraq and welcomed by Israel, namely that they should leave their ancestral homes, and become penniless refugees in a country about which they knew very little. By 1951 the community was no more.

When Artaxerxes II issued his decree ordering Ezra to go to Judea, he specified that only those who were minded of their own free will to go up to Jerusalem should accompany him. How ironical therefore that the operation, organized by Israel, which transported from Baghdad to the transit camps in Israel the disoriented and bewildered multitude of their descendants who – to quote the Book of Jonah – were then scarcely able to discern between their right hand and their left hand (Jonah, 4:11), should have been officially called Operation 'Ezra and Nehemiah'.

Elie Kedourie: An Overview

P. J. VATIKIOTIS

Elie Kedourie's work on the history and politics of the modern Middle East went so much counter to the established versions that some of his detractors sought to dismiss him as a solitary academic who regretted not only the destruction of the Ottoman imperial state but also the dissolution of the British Empire. Both processes, Kedourie argued, were the result of deliberate and cumulative acts by well-meaning, albeit misguided, policy-makers in the West in general and in England in particular. He used much of his scholarly talent from the mid-1950s to the mid-1970s to document and define these Western misconceptions.

His first book, *England and the Middle East: The Destruction of the Ottoman Empire*, published in 1956, was the first major elaboration of this view.[1] It was followed twenty years later in 1976 by *In the Anglo-Arab Labyrinth*. This was a detailed analysis of the McMahon-Husayn Correspondence of 1915–16. Puzzled as he was by the contradiction and the incongruence between the assumptions and the record of British policy and the political and social reality of Middle Eastern societies, Kedourie persevered in the study of the conduct of British officials and their motives when formulating policy, and the arrangements for the political future of the Middle East after the First World War. He ventured at the same time into a close study of Middle Eastern personalities whether Arab nationalists or religious leaders and reformers, many of whom were British protégés, and discovered that they provided a far more realistic and therefore reliable criterion for understanding the nature of politics and political conduct in the Middle East. He also saw this study as more revealing of the Middle Easterner's perception of power, his preferences for traditional politics and the Islamic political idiom and ethic, and finally displaying his stubborn failure to devise and implement a constitutional European-style representative political system beyond the superficial adoption of its formal scaffolding.[2]

Having discovered so many inconsistencies and suspect interpretations in the existing presentations, Kedourie concluded that there was something amiss in the agenda for the study of the area as formulated and promoted by British officials and policy-makers. He set out to demonstrate how unrealistic and misleading this was. He did this by examining factors such as Arab nationalists and revolutionary leaders and rulers. He came to argue both comfortably and convincingly that Arab nationalism and Arab unity as fostered by the British Foreign Office were not the *force motrice* but that the reality was to be found rather in the regional and local conflicts and in the pursuit of personal ambition by a variety of Arab rulers and politicians. He demonstrated that the examination of indigenous forces, including local politicians and their conduct on the ground, was more fruitful than the scheme devised by outsiders, be they great powers or not. *The Chatham House Version*, a volume of collected essays published in 1970, was crucial in depicting the glaring difference between the Foreign Office and its adherents and the more indigenous versions of the Middle East in the inter-war period. Followed by the publication of yet another collection of essays in 1974, *Arabic Political Memoirs*, Kedourie now formulated a wholly new approach to Middle Eastern studies, at any rate in Britain, different and diametrically opposed to the one that held sway from the end of the First World War.[3]

There have been those who contended that Elie Kedourie established a 'London School of Middle Eastern Studies'. This belief was popular among aspiring research students, and particularly those who, despite the attraction of graduate study in the United States, still preferred to come to the United Kingdom, to the School of Oriental and African Studies (SOAS), the London School of Economics and Political Science (LSE) or Oxford, where they would either be supervised by Kedourie or failing that have access to him. Kedourie was too private and retiring a scholar to have recognized such a school, let alone to have thought of himself as its founder or leader. As his near exact contemporary in the University of London, at the SOAS (1965–90) I was never aware of a 'Kedourie school', but only of a Kedourie approach to the study of the Middle East with which I sympathized and to the main contentions of which I subscribed. I had arrived at the same conclusions via an independent, though parallel, route of political philosophy, heavily dependent on the Classics, but also affected by a brush with the ideological politics of Muslim heretical sects and movements of the ninth to the eleventh centuries, as well as through contemporary Arabic literature.

One can aver that although Kedourie may not have founded a particular 'School of Middle Eastern Studies', he did have a general impact on the wider study of the region beyond his own particular research interests and output. This judgement becomes more acute when one looks at his output between 1990 and his premature death two years later. Some of this work was published posthumously. Much of it was written after retirement, while on visiting appointments away from London. It included his writings about wider themes in general politics and political thought. One can see here the link between Kedourie's deeper interests in the disciplines of history and political theory and his more empirical work about the Middle East.[4]

Kedourie's analytical work on the Middle East is significantly informed and influenced by his wider intellectual formation, by his acquaintance with European medieval political history and thought, as well as by his understanding of the Enlightenment and the French Revolution and their numerous consequences in both East and the West.[5]

Those of us for whom the study of political thought and political philosophy, including the Classics, had been a central part of our formal university training were naturally attracted to the new Kedourie approach to the study of the modern Middle East. We had already found the Italian Machiavelli school of politics more relevant in understanding the politics of the area than the typical post-Enlightenment approach, be it progressive positivist, Marxist or other. What was also significant was the fact that in our generation, there was no elaborate, highly structured university training in what came to be known as Middle Eastern Studies. What was available to us in postgraduate university programmes was the study of politics, history, economics and literature mainly of the European or Western world. Our most relevant and perhaps strongest qualification in subsequently studying the Middle East was our knowledge of one or more of its main languages – Arabic, Hebrew, Turkish or Persian, sometimes combined with our provenance from that part of the world.

Many in the field, especially among the establishment of state officials and university teachers, still considered Kedourie an isolated voice of peripheral influence and would deny that his work had a systematic and cumulative impact on the study of the wider Middle Eastern region. Some academics, it has been alleged, advised their students not to read his work. But none of them in their *fthonos* – to use the classical word for envy and spite – reckoned with his more stunning work yet to come. While all the pundits among them celebrated the collapse of communism and their impending role in making democrats out of their charges in the Middle East, Kedourie published a book, and a posthumous article.[6] He argued, in his usual devastating and analytically detailed style, that this kind of political system would simply not work in the Middle East, historically a major centre of oriental despotism and of repeatedly failed attempts at the construction of constitutional government. He again raised the spectre of a local culture and a religious faith that were and remained inhospitable, if not hostile, to open, pluralistic, constitutionally representative or democratic political systems. Perhaps one of the more significant intellectual legacies of Kedourie's impact on the study of the Middle East is the axiom that there is no redemption or salvation in politics. This, I suspect, carried over from his study of political thought and philosophy.

One corroborating instance of Kedourie's wider impact on the study of the Middle East is the scandal occasioned by the scurrilous anonymous review of my book *Conflict in the Middle East* (1971) in the *Times Literary Supplement* of December 1971, where the reviewer objected specifically to 'the author's association with members of such underprivileged minorities of the Middle East as Elie Kedourie'. The reviewer, in short, was using his review of my book gratuitously to attack Kedourie, revealing the extent and degree of envy and malice against him.

His *Politics in the Middle East*,[7] is a lucid and coherent statement about the nature of politics in the Middle East from the end of the First World War to the end of the Gulf War. After a long introduction where he writes about the region's Islamic and Ottoman legacy of 'gaps and separation – between ruler and ruled, between town and country, between the nomad and settled population, between religious communities' and of despotism, citing A.H. Lybyer's famous dichotomy of the Ruling Institution and the Religious Institution,[8] Kedourie assesses the nature and magnitude of the threat and predicament that the modern world constitutes for the region's rulers and their societies. He then proceeds to argue closely that constitutionalism has failed in one after another of the Middle Eastern states, and to conclude that what has taken hold as the preferred political idiom is ideological politics, including extreme variants of nationalism and religious fanaticism or fundamentalism, in short millennial or millenarian politics.

The widespread clamour and mindless talk among our colleagues after the collapse of communism, that Middle Eastern states, regimes and rulers were now anxious to develop, in consonance with developments in Europe, open, pluralist free market economies and thus move rapidly towards democratic political systems, got the following response from Kedourie. He argued that there was no evidence of how all this could happen without open, tolerant polities of competing groups and interests under some form of representative arrangement guaranteed by a constitutional order which, among other things, limited the arbitrary power of the ruler and rendered him accountable to some constituency.

This conundrum led him to write the last two works before his sudden and premature death in June 1992. One, an article, 'Democracy and the Third World: Governance of Developing Countries',[9] reminded students of the area that 'Democracy signifies representative government by representatives of the people, according to a constitution' and that 'representative government implied not only elections and votes, but also the neutrality of the state in matters of belief particularly religious belief'. Whereas such a system promoted the dispersal of power, the political tradition of oriental despotism in Asia and Africa encouraged the concentration of power in one ruler, a difference really between modern and primitive government

He discussed these differences and difficulties in greater detail in his other, his last monograph, *Democracy and Arab Political Culture*. He reiterated here the long-standing position of an antithesis between Middle Eastern culture and a particular kind of polity or political system invented and developed in western Europe, a successor to the earlier political structure of the Greek polis or city-state.

This then is a broad overview of Kedourie's approach to and discussion of various aspects of the modern history and politics of the Middle East. It shows his unmistakable impact on the study of the region, an impact I might add which has yet to be challenged. Short of a miraculous and rapid emergence of constitutional representative governments in the region which would by definition overthrow the Kedourie version, his intellectual position is bound to prevail for the foreseeable future.

NOTES

1. First published by Bowes and Bowes in 1956; then in 1978 by Harvester Press. A later edition, published by Mansell in 1986, contains a new introduction relating the circumstances of the oral examination of his thesis presented for the D.Phil examination at Oxford.
2. See his monograph *Afghani and 'Abduh: An Essay on Religious Unbelief and Political Activism in Modern Islam* (London: Frank Cass, 1966), which led some of his critics to describe Kedourie as a moralist. And yet this book was the first of its kind in suggesting that 'things aren't what they seem' in the Middle East. It encouraged the deeper digging, more searching inquiry into the personal, social, political background and record of so-called religious reformers and national activists and rebels. It brought the whole religious reform movement into question, and offered serious reservations over its nature, the motives and objectives of its leaders. See also his collection of essays, *Islam in the Modern World* (London, 1980), esp. pp.1–84.
3. *The Chatham House Version and Other Middle Eastern Studies* (London, 1970); *Arabic Political Memoirs and Other Studies* (London, 1974) contains his elaborate views on political parties and factions, originally a major entry in the second edition of the *Encyclopaedia of Islam* under *hizb*; also the fate of constitutionalism in the region and other seminal studies.
4. See his 'Arnold J. Toynbee, History as Paradox' in *The Crossman Confessions and Other Essays on Politics, History and Religion* (London, 1984), pp.192–206, and 'Religion and Politics, Arnold Toynbee and Martin Wight', ibid., pp.207–18. See also 'The Chatham House Version' in *The Chatham House Version* ... , pp.351–94; *Nationalism in Asia and Africa* (London, 1970).
5. See the essays on Jews and Judaism in *The Crossman Confessions*, pp.219–50 and 85–190.
6. *Democracy and Arab Political Culture*, 2nd ed. (London, 1994), 'Democracy and the Third World: Governance for Developing Countries' in *International Journal on World Peace*, Vol.xi, No.1, March 1994, pp.7–16.
7. Oxford University Press, 1992.
8. *The Government of the Ottoman Empire in the Time of Suleyman the Magnificant* (Harvard University Press, 1913).
9. See Proceedings of the Euro-Arab Seminar, 'Euro-Arab Understanding and Cultural Exchange', Council of Europe, Strasbourg 14–15 Nov. 1991.

A Personal Note

MICHAEL LEIFER

I came to the LSE in the mid-1950s as a research student. The first person I met was Dr Anne Bohm who was then the Secretary of the Graduate School. She put me in touch with the late Charles Manning through whose initiative I first came into contact with Elie Kedourie. To my good fortune, he eventually became my joint supervisor at the School although I was located in another department to his own.

My experience of being supervised by Elie was awesome, daunting and highly rewarding. As an ill-informed research student, I was acutely conscious of the weight and range of learning which he brought to the supervision and especially of his steely powers of intellect which were applied rigorously to weak arguments and imperfect draft chapters. Elie was a demanding mentor who took it for granted that his instructions would be diligently observed. The message was quite simple; research requires disciplined dedication. However daunting to this student, Elie was also a great intellectual benefactor. The experience of being supervised by him was rich, formative and long-lasting. It was from Elie that I learned at first-hand the values that should inform the life of an academic community. It was from him also that I acquired a fuller understanding of the activity of politics and what might be expected of those who indulged in it. I like to think that such an understanding gleaned from tutorial conversations has stood me in good stead during my own academic career in interpreting a regional field of study different from that which originally brought me under Elie's intellectual influence.

Elie Kedourie was not a man of many words beyond his voluminous distinguished writings. His instruction and advice tended to be conveyed in a laconic style; short, pithy and penetrating observations were characteristic of his manner of communication. And when he communicated in that way, the face of the outwardly taciturn teacher who epitomized gravitas would more often than not explode into a smile revealing a great warmth of spirit behind the mask of scholarship. As a supervisor, Elie was not only a demanding and stimulating mentor acting always in students' best interests but also a strong source of support for them from which I benefited greatly, to my everlasting gratitude. Indeed, that support was critical in my own case.

When I later came to join the staff of the School, Elie was ever friendly and helpful. I was a member of a different department and I had changed my academic interests so that our intellectual paths crossed only intermittently. As a colleague, however, he was always responsive to requests and advice as when, for example, he gave up time at the weekend to come to talk to students of my own department at a conference in Windsor Great Park. As a colleague, he also sustained a reputation for academic integrity for which he was highly respected both within and beyond the LSE. He was not someone to be influenced by the latest academic fashions but had an unwavering sense of where he stood and what he stood for. He believed in the independence of the academic community and made his strong views widely known about the changing adverse relationship between that community and government.

Our last communication took place when, after his retirement, I had pleasure in writing to him in Washington to offer my congratulations on his appointment to CBE. He replied with some kind words and good advice on how I might use to the advantage of the LSE a position of administrative responsibility which I had recently assumed. He wrote in the best interests of the School to which he had devoted the greater part of his academic life and to which he made such a distinguished contribution.

A View from Academe

KENNETH MINOGUE

A Memorial Meeting is a celebration of individuality, and in the case of Elie Kedourie, there is a great deal to celebrate. Both in his scholarly work, and in his membership of his university, Elie was highly distinctive.

He was also enigmatic, something symbolized by the fact that the world at large often hesitated between Alie and Ellie. Part of this enigmatic character was the result of his Baghdad childhood.

One basic constituent, I should guess, was an immense admiration for England which he acquired early on, and which was part of the imaginative sympathy he had with Michael Oakeshott, who was in one sense the archetypal Englishman. This admiration for England – England rather than Britain, I think – was central because the Britain he came to in the late 1940s was in decline. His overpowering sense of this decline concerned nothing so vulgar as the loss of empire. Rather, it was a loss of nerve stemming from a variety of sources, including particularly the currency of doctrines of historical guilt for empire. Such doctrines, Elie thought, were especially prevalent in upper-class intellectual life, and gave to much British statesmanship a quality of self-indulgence which led to many evils abroad. This was the cast of mind he criticized in *The Chatham House Version and Other Essays*. In his response to the separatist pressures of nationalism, he became an intellectual centurion.

A good example of his view of the corruption of the process of government in Britain itself can be found in his essay 'The Crossman Confessions' which became the title of a collection published in 1984. Rejecting with the bitter irony of which he was a master the opinion that British civil servants promoted the interests of their own class, he added:

> The reality is that for at least four decades now – ever since the outbreak of the Second World War – the civil service has acquired habits which have ended by becoming ingrained. It has learnt the ambition to fine-tune the economy, to manage demand, and control supply, and bestow on each citizen no more and no less than his fair share of income – or rather of pocket money – and of 'welfare'; to be, in one word, for the British people what their counterparts in the Indian civil service had been for the ryot: a very father and mother (pp.4–5).

This passage illustrates one central feature of Elie's treatment of British politics: that a sense of the dangers of oriental despotism is always to be found in the background. He hardly ever used terms like 'liberty' and 'freedom', but a love of what they signify governs his attitude to civilization.

There is, however, a deeper dimension to his disillusion with the world in which he found himself. My impression of Elie is of someone whose moral sense was a continuing beacon in his decisions. A certain moral fastidiousness, no less than scholarly integrity distanced him from the popular political enthusiasms of his time. In remarks he made when retiring from the Government Department, he remembered an incident from a classroom in his youth:

> I cannot remember what the subject or the question was, but I still see the tall, gangling schoolboy standing up at his desk and telling our master with the self-assured smile of someone imparting a potent revelation, that freedom is the recognition of necessity. I suppose he must have got this from some penny dreadful by some Palme Dutt or other ... For this hectoring doctrine I felt an aversion ...

In later years, this attitude comes up, for example, in a disdain for British cabinet ministers discussing a Middle Eastern question, such as the British withdrawal from Aden, or the Gulf, not in terms of the commitments violated, promises broken or the realities of national interest but of the immediate political advantage of shedding an expensive responsibility, whatever the consequences may have been for a population handed over to what he did not hesitate to call a gang of terrorists.

Calling a spade a spade was found by Elie to be entirely compatible with scholarship. Robert Conquest has recently been complaining about academic students of the Soviet Union turning into moral idiots from a mechanical conception of scholarly neutrality and impartiality. Elie knew exactly what he meant. On the other hand, I have never known anyone more scrupulous about matching his historical conclusions with the available evidence. One of his most characteristic contributions to discussion was shrugging his shoulders and saying: 'How can we know?'

'How can we know?' is a philosopher's question, and he was the master of a philosophical sophistication all the more formidable because he wore it lightly. He was as crisply oracular in this as in all other fields. I remember many years ago when G.E. Moore and the analytic tradition of philosophy were being discussed. 'They are bookkeepers,' remarked Elie, meaning that their philosophy was merely shuffling phenomena back and forth between concepts. I once mentioned to him the lucubration of Gurdijieff and Ouspensky. As usual, he was familiar with them. 'It is treacle,' he said.

One would be inclined to judge him an historian, but this would fail to do justice to the breadth of his culture. His prose, for example. I have always thought that there was something Conradian about it. Its liveliness was quite un-English, it was precise in its utterance, and produced occasional delightful shocks as he exploited a word found in his explorations, but seldom visited in the indolent patois of the native.

This liveliness of style was often enriched by his immersions in the poets. Eliot and Paul Valéry were particular favourites, but the French classicists and others also made their appearance. Indeed, so far as Britain and France were concerned, Elie was culturally ambidextrous, and I have always thought we were lucky to get him. He recalled (in his retirement remarks) seeing an advertisement for the School in the *New Statesman*, and off went his application. I count the School very lucky to have acquired him. He could easily have become an adornment of the Seine rather than the Thames.

He taught here at the School for 37 years, and was a loyal LSE man. He appreciated the virtues of collegiality. He was, indeed, often abroad but when his turn came to perform required duties – being convenor, serving on the time-consuming standing sub-committee of the Appointments Committee –he did not flinch.

There was, perhaps, good reason why he might have done so. He must have known, as those who knew him certainly did, that this was a remarkable mind whose riches could barely be fully explored in several lifetimes. He might well have taken the view that what he most had to give the world was his scholarship rather than the underlabouring of keeping it going. But his moral sense came into play.

His method, as it were, was to use his teaching to master a theme and then to develop it at his leisure in a book. This was how *Nationalism* was created. Its marvellous lucidity includes a sentence which in retrospect looks programmatic:

> … what now seems natural once was unfamiliar, needing argument, persuasion, evidences of many kinds; what seems simple and transparent is really obscure and contrived, the outcome of circumstances now forgotten and preoccupations now academic, the residue of metaphysical systems sometimes incompatible and even contradictory. To elucidate this doctrine it is necessary to enquire into the fortunes of certain ideas in the philosophical tradition of Europe, and how they came to prominence at this particular period (pp.9–10).

His work on Middle Eastern politics grew in the same way, and so did his work on Hegel. Many of us remember going along to a set text class he gave on *The Philosophy of Right* and this transmuted into 15 lectures on Hegel and Marx – that is to say, 14 on Hegel, and one on Marx – now published as a book. This was a form of composition which made up in thoroughness what it lost in speed.

I never knew a man less harassed by a deadline, or so it always seemed. Yet the record shows that he often did write for an occasion, so he must have been. The secret was, however, that he always wrote from within himself, out of the abundant resources of a vast knowledge of the character and biographies of individuals in a political situation, and of reports, documents and memoranda.

Further, his sense of duty sometimes impelled him to divert his energies into issues of policy. He took very seriously the catastrophic changes in British higher education since the Robbins Report, and was persuaded to turn aside to write pamphlets on this threat – a threat whose operation on the School here was by no means the least of the materials of disillusion in his later years. *Diamonds into Glass* and *Perestroika in the Universities* are among the best things on the current academic catastrophe.

Elie's university – his LSE as it were – was the place he joined as a teacher in the 1950s, when universities allowed leisure and reflection, and he could enjoy the conversation of friends like Michael Oakeshott, Martin Wight and many others, many of them still happily with us. In those days, the Common Room was filled for morning and afternoon tea. I dare say the conversation was not all pure gold, but it wasted time less horribly than fulfilling the demands of committees and submitting to the management of research.

A scholar, fortunately, lives on in his books, and Elie's will come to be recognized as both historical and literary classics, just as he will take his place among the most original minds the School has been fortunate to have in its first hundred years. We however will also remember a strikingly handsome presence, a kindly reserve and an amused chuckle at the more outrageous follies of public life.

Beyond Academe

REGINA ALLEN

When we saw the news of Elie's CBE in the paper, Sam, my husband, sent a fax of congratulation to Washington, to save time letting him know how pleased we were. In due course we received a note from him which said, 'the best thing about it is the good wishes of one's friends' – of whom I know there are very many the world over. I am only able to speak for myself and, maybe, a little, for Sam and my daughter. That was a typically understated response, but clearly Elie was pleased to be able to invite some people to tea at University College when he came to receive the CBE and lecture on 'Politics and the Academy' at UC the next day. It was one of the last times we saw him and the lecture was, of course, fascinating. The last time was a long relaxed Sunday lunch, at our house, when we were looking forward to Sylvia and Elie coming back to spend most of their time in London.

I remember the first time we met still vividly although it was 45 years ago at their wedding. Sam had come back from the RAF to finish his degree and he and Elie graduated at the same time in 1950. (I had finished earlier – not having been away – and we had been married a year). There was a deep impression of a rare quality in both of them which is still with me. We knew then that Elie was someone unusual and very special.

The friendship became one that included all four of us and then our children and has gone on into the second generation. It was always an event to look forward to when we were to see them and, in the nature of things, these are memories of lots of meals – festive and informal. We have a picture of a picnic by the river at Oxford when Elie was at St Antony's, but there are many more pictures in my mind; April 1986, sitting on the steps of a public building in Concorde eating a tuna 'sub' and talking about American history. Both Elie and Sylvia were teaching at Brandeis at the time, and the next morning at breakfast over Armenian bread he gave us, to quote a phrase used by Alan Beattie, 'a calm, assured and highly intelligent dissection' of the current British political situation.

I remember dinner on a warm August night by the Serpentine to celebrate their 40th wedding anniversary. Around that time too there were fish and chips in their kitchen, after we had gleefully used our travel passes to get cheap matinee theatre seats. On these occasions we talked about anything because he was interested in everything. The 'terrifying incapacity for small talk' mentioned in Professor Minogue's obituary, means to me that nothing remained trivial because the talk was so interesting.

The intervals had been longer in recent years, because of Elie's travels to visiting professorships and accepting various honours, most of which we only heard about afterwards, if at all. I looked at his *Who's Who* entry for the first time when he died and was amazed at what it contained!

Our meetings were usually full of laughter – which one might not guess from some of the things that have been written about him. I always think of him smiling and listening carefully to what one said in answer to a question or comment. Because of the breadth of his learning and the clarity of his vision he also had a breadth of sympathy which made it possible for him to listen to a different kind of language, and respect the basis in experience of quite other modes of thought. This was not from an abstract concept about rights to opinion but something I felt as well as understood when with him.

I suppose I am one of 'those of liberal and progressive disposition' to whom exposure to Elie could be 'shocking' – to quote Alan Beattie again. Not a bit – I was never shocked by him! He laughed at me for my optimism and my addiction to trying earnestly to improve all sorts of situations (I became a social worker on leaving LSE and have remained in that field), as well as various inter-faith and inter-cultural activities, but I never felt that laughter to be unkind. In fact I never knew him to be unkind or angry. I felt that he approved of my trying, however unsuccessfully, and that what he did do was help me to clarify my own thinking in explaining to him 'What does that mean?'. He could be very illuminating in return. To quote another obituary, he was 'high minded without being censorious' about the kinds of people and problems I have had to relate to. He once denied, with surprise, the suggestion, that he thought me woolly-minded and that was as gratifying, coming from him, as a florid compliment from someone else.

I believe he was a man of strong and fine feelings, although he never used the language of emotion. This was implicit in his courtesy and consideration for the feelings of others.

It has been important to me to try and find the right words to talk about this man whose use of English was so precise, creative, elegant – and funny! No doubt this was so in the other languages he wrote and spoke as well.

It has been hard for us to remember not to store up questions and requests for clarification of political situations everywhere for our next meeting. He explained so that one understood – *never* to demonstrate his own knowledge. I wish I had been at LSE later, or gone back, to be taught by him.

It has been a source of great encouragement as well as pleasure to us to have retained Elie's and Sylvia's affection over all these years. We never talked about that – it was as though we all took it for granted, but *we* never did.

I would venture to say that we shared, and share still, 'inarticulate major assumptions' – to quote Laski – about what is important in life (although we certainly, even when we were young, never sat around talking about the meaning of life). That is, that what in the end matters most along with truth and justice, is enduring, loving, personal and family relationships. Nobody who knows Sylvia and Elie can doubt the truth of that. George, when he spoke at the Memorial Service at Bevis Marks, referred to the dedication of one of Elie's early books, characteristically, to S. with a Biblical reference which is part of the tribute to the woman of worth – 'The heart of her husband doth safely trust in her'...

I am not given to Biblical quotation but I found another in my diary – while looking for a theatre date with Sylvia – it is from Ecclesiastes: 'A faithful friend is a life giving medicine and those who fear the Lord will find one. Whoever fears the Lord makes true friends, for as a person is so is their friend'.

I would profoundly wish that I could be like him.

A Master All His Own

DAVID PRYCE-JONES

I would have preferred to improvise those few well-chosen words which some people seem able to call upon on such an occasion as this. To put thoughts on paper is to risk the obituary mode, and I fear the autobiographical; but at least I may get closer to expressing, with more of a *mot juste*, what is in my mind and heart about Elie, whom I consider altogether exceptional, indeed, a great man.

I was once in the position to commission him to write reviews as I came to know him, which was a privilege. Elie's demeanour was grave and courtly, until there broke that sudden burst of delighted laughter at some story which revealed the truth, whether about the follies of some particular person, probably a politician or a journalist, or the folly of mankind. His laughter signified not only understanding of the world as it is, but that acceptance of reality which is wisdom. It was extraordinary that experience and learning, which in others might have fed bitterness, in Elie fed generosity and understanding. In my day, the schools and universities of this country formed rather an efficient plant for processing the raw material of youth. Unsuspecting boys and girls went into one end of this plant and emerged as standardized as sausages, knowing all the answers but none of the questions, amid much congratulation on holding opinions which for no very good reason were considered progressive. In this best of all possible worlds, so it appeared, a wonderful brand-new welfare system had been created in which we were all to be free and equal and creative, at no cost to anyone else. Contributing to this wonder was the withdrawal from Empire, which would allow everyone else to follow the British lead and be as free, equal and creative as we were. Violence and war belonged to the past: even the Soviet lion would in the end prove to be another British lamb.

The shock of *The Chatham House Version* is still with me. I must stand for many people when I say that my perceptions afterwards will never be the same again. In the dim and stagnant pond which British intellectual life had then become, at last there was a living creature. First, the language. More than a scholar, Elie was an artist, a master of English prose, that greatest of vehicles for telling sober truths soberly; a classic vehicle for the description of the particular so as to illuminate the general. No doubt the English language suited Elie's temperament, but it was surely a matter of fortune that someone from his background should come to write in it. And then, the subject matter. Evidently, this was not the best of all possible worlds. The views which our elders and betters had been indoctrinating in us were widely complacent and completely self-serving. Britain had acquired historic responsibilities which it had evidently failed to discharge; and much present disaster originated from that fact. Matters in which we congratulated ourselves were actually dereliction, a failure, sometimes of policy and sometimes of plain human feelings for other people. Destruction and death were the consequences of these failures, which had to be studied if they were not to be repeated; and to remind myself of reality I often re-read the essay in that volume entitled 'Minorities', a masterpiece in its simultaneous grasp of events and empathy for others. It is notoriously hard to evaluate how public opinion coalesces, or why it then changes; but I believe that Elie, through his combination of moral passion and learning, obliged people to re-evaluate the events concerned with the end of Empire, and to form sounder and juster views of the received wisdom of the day. Empire was not merely the exploitation of those incapable of resisting. It was also law and order, and the application of settled and universal standards of civility. The collapse of Empire, whether Hapsburg, Ottoman or British, also entailed an end to the settled and universal standards of that empire. In the case of Britain, and this was something Elie drove home, there was no way that the people of the Empire could have predicted how an apparently great and powerful government in London, triumphant in world wars, would leave them in the lurch the moment that it judged that it was in its interest to do so. The tyranny under which many of these people still live is a matter of local culture and custom to be sure, but it is also the consequence of mistaken policy in capitals which should have known better. How those decisions came to be taken, and the consequent benign or fatal interactions between ruler and ruled, was Elie's subject matter.

Once, I asked him how he ordered his own notes, since he was able to call upon so much material gathered first hand from the archives. 'Oh, on pieces of paper stuffed into brown envelopes' was the answer; and it gives hope to lesser scholars. In depicting minutely the very many vain, ambitious and foolish men who made political processes what they were, he did not just throw up his hands in horror, for that would have put him on much the same footing as those running the youth sausage factory: merely another complainer that the British had never done anything right. On the contrary, he insisted that, in the position of the decision-makers, we might have done no better. But the world is unregenerate and ideals cannot be reconciled: but because there are so few philosopher-kings, if any, does not mean that there are no lessons. Identification with the victims was natural. But it is the sense of pity, of loss and waste aroused by the whole process of history, which infuses and vitalizes Elie's work, as it does any true artist establishing the claim to greatness.

An Israeli View

ITAMAR RABINOVICH

In May 1991, during the annual session of its Board of Governors, Tel Aviv University bestowed on Elie Kedourie an honorary doctorate. As the Rector of the University at that time, I delivered a short speech during the ceremony, and I was very much tempted to tell the audience the story of the original doctorate that Elie never received. By that time it had ceased to be gossip and it had become a matter of record, when Elie, in the introduction to the new edition of *England and the Middle East*, published his part of the correspondence with the Oxford authorities at the time. Very typical of Elie, he would never publish somebody else's letter, but he published his side of the correspondence: and I thought the better of it. The 600 people in the auditorium during an annual Board of Governors did not strike me as the appropriate audience for listening to this significant but intricate story, but about a year later, in spring 1992, during another important occasion at the life of the University, the granting of doctorates, it struck me that this would be the right occasion. Speaking to a hundred fresh Ph.D.s from Tel Aviv University, it occurred to me that it might be the right message to that particular audience to tell them of a man who was not willing to compromise his truth in order to obtain a doctorate. Somewhat ironically for about a hundred young men and women who at that moment thought that the most precious thing on earth they were about to obtain was the Ph.D.: but the story went down well with that audience, and so much so that it was reported in the Israeli press at the time. I clipped the story and sent it to Elie and Sylvia in Washington, only to be informed by Sylvia a few days later in a tearful voice that it arrived a day too late for Elie to have enjoyed it.

Now I chose to begin by telling you this story because it illustrates the three dimensions of Elie's personality and life that I want to describe: Elie the scholar; the Israeli and Jewish dimension of Elie's life; and Elie the man and the friend.

The scholarship was of course recognized by us when we decided to bestow on him an honorary Ph.D. Much was said by my colleagues here at the head table about Elie the intellectual and Elie the scholar, and I would not wish either to belabour the issue or to repeat some of what was said; but I think the evening will not be complete if I did not offer you an assessment of Elie's contribution to Middle Eastern studies in the latter part of the century. One cannot envisage Middle Eastern studies in the 1950s, 1960s, 1970s, 1980s and today without Elie's hand, and along with him, Sylvia's contribution. Elie left after him a *corpus*, the books, the essays: and the *corpus* has its own place, and has had a great impact, and, I think, will continue to have a great impact upon the field. One could disagree with Elie. One did not have to accept his view or his opinion on a particular issue, but one could not ignore it. One had to come to grips with Elie's opinion: one could choose to take another view, but one had to take it into account. And when one reviews the scope of issues covered by Elie – in the formative period of British policy towards the Middle East during the First World War and during the peace settlement; the role of Islam in the political life of the region; Arab nationalism; the Arab–Israeli conflict; American policies; parliamentarianism; constitutionalism; political parties and Young Turks – and if we remember that he left an important *corpus* of work on British politics and political philosophy, it was indeed an amazing achievement and of great impact on our field and other fields. To this we should add the journal which became, and remains, the single most important and influential journal in the field; and the generation, or generations, of students in Middle Eastern studies who continue the work. One can recognize an Elie Kedourie Ph.D. We have heard a bit about the instruction: and the results are evident. There is a whole school of young scholars and now older scholars, professors, who have been formed by Elie and continue to preach that particular message and to exercise that influence on the field.

Now the Jewish and Israeli dimension. Elie was a traditional, proud Jew; and a proud Iraqi Jew. I think that for Elie as a Jew, the life of the Jewish community in Baghdad in the earlier decades of this century could have been the most satisfactory model. There was some anger in him about the forces which brought that life to an end. British policy, Arab nationalism and Zionism among them. But being a wise and pragmatic man, Elie made his peace with Zionism: Israel came into being, it became a central fact of Jewish life; and even if, intellectually, Elie could not be defined as a Zionist, he developed a warm relationship to and with the State of Israel, and this relationship manifested itself primarily through his relationship with the universities and with us. Yes, there were other aspects to it. He was very much interested in the work of the Centre for the Study of Iraqi Jewry near Tel Aviv. Yes, he was the intellectual luminary when he visited. People sought his opinion. Political leaders wanted to hear what Elie had to say about this trend and that development. The newspapers were always after him. But the main focus of the at least yearly visit, sometimes two visits a year, to the various universities, was academic life – a conference, a lecture, a meeting with students, a meeting with colleagues. To this extent we all were his disciples, even if we studied with someone else and had our Ph.D. from another university. One could be a disciple without being a student: and, if I am allowed to do it, I would like to define myself, not just as a friend, but also as a disciple in that sense of the word.

Now, Elie the man and the friend. What one admired in the act of a young Elie Kedourie – defying the Oxford establishment, willing to pay a price for his truth – is a quality that remained throughout. The search for the truth – the principle, the thing that Elie believed in – was something he was willing to stand for and to pay a price for. It was a quality, a propensity, which has always evoked admiration as being just one of the formative qualities of a remarkable personality. But Elie was also a good friend. I mentioned many visits to Israel and to Israeli universities. We in Tel Aviv always wanted to believe that we were Elie's favourites, that there was a particular relationship and a particular friendship between the Kedouries and Tel Aviv University. Elie came to Tel Aviv when our Middle Eastern Studies Centre, the Department and the Research Institute, were in their infancy: in 1969. Not much to see, perhaps not much to believe in, but it was love at first sight, mutual, and Elie continued to come and to invest in us; and I believe that as we grew and developed, something of that investment was returned by us. The attitude to students, not only when they were supervised but later on: Elie believed in his better students and sometimes there was a conflict. He believed in truth and he was loyal to his students; and when he had to recommend a student who was not among his best, one could see the conflict of emotions: the loyalty, and the quest for truth. In his elegant and eloquent way, Elie always found a way of being fair to his students without being unfair to those who asked him about it. But fortunately, most of those who were able to finish their dissertations with Elie were first class; these conflicts were very rare. Elie was an exemplary teacher, when the students studied with him and under him and further, as they were looking for positions, as they were looking for publishers, and as they had to be guided further along the way.

I have described three aspects or three dimensions of a life and a personality: but one could see the underlying unity. There was unity to Elie's personality, and there was a fullness to that personality: and these aspects, and others that I could mention, while being diverse, all comply with that fullness and with that unity. He is sorely missed.

A Ph.D. Experience

LIORA LUKITZ

The decision to engage in a Ph.D. programme came to me relatively late, and was clouded by doubts regarding the effort, time and costs involved. However, I did not have any doubts concerning whom I should ask to supervise me in the project I wished to undertake. Professor Elie Kedourie seemed to me best suited amongst the leading authorities in the field, and the one who would agree to guide me through the complexities of a project focusing on 'majorities' and 'minorities' and their interplay within Iraq's political context.

Already then, I was a great admirer of the courage with which he addressed the most thorny questions of Middle East history and politics, and was especially familiar with his seminal chapters, 'Continuity and Change in Modern Iraqi History' (*Asian Affairs*, 1975), and 'The Kingdom of Iraq: A Retrospect' (*The Chatham House Version and Other Middle Eastern Studies*, New York: Praeger, 1970). Both chapters had become established landmarks in Iraq's historiography for their incisive analysis of the monarchy and its institutions. The scope of these works went beyond internal affairs, extending to the ideological frame of the Ba'th regime, and defining the guidelines of Iraq's foreign policy: Iraqi–Iranian rivalry for supremacy in the Gulf area, the Kurdish problem, the attempts to annex Kuwait (1938–39, 1961), and the instigation of a movement in Syria in favour of union with Iraq.

Pan-Arab ideology in foreign affairs, and Arabism in internal ones, the two sources of the Ba'thist doctrinal approach implemented after the Ba'th rise to power in 1963, were merely variations on the ideology disseminated by the monarchical regime. There was continuity in an aggressive foreign policy, and there was continuity in an oppressive internal one dictated by 'the strain to which an extremely heterogeneous society was subjected by a powerful centralizing government'.[1] 'There it is', I thought to myself, turning all other explanations into mere variants on the main theme. The usurpation of power by a small conspiratorial group, the establishment of an extensive centralized power, the stifling of any oppositional organization, instability and violence as patterns of political behaviour, transmitted as they were from one regime to another.

The underlying motif in both chapters was the search for the roots of Iraq's instability, and tracing the way in which a determined historical development could be defined by the sequence of events leading up to it.

'The Kingdom of Iraq: A Retrospect' gave a more detailed study of the monarchy and the way in which Iraq's specific problems influenced the shaping of Iraq's political culture. Preceding 'Continuity and Change', which pointed to the logical conclusion of patterns established in the past, 'The Kingdom of Iraq' focused on the very tendencies in government and society already evident during the monarchy. With its heterogeneous population, formed in its majority by Shiis and Kurds, who never enjoyed power commensurate with their importance', Iraq spelled trouble from the very beginning. Ethnic and religious animosities, controlled only by the instruments of an extremist ideology, would remain Iraq's main problem. Was it all obvious from the outset?

Upheavals in state formation, reactions of a tribal population to attempts at centralism, the rise of the army as a political factor, and the initial oscillation between pan-Arabism and regional integration (embodied, among others, by the 1936 Sidqi-Sulaiman cabinet) were only some of the issues explored. Other focus on the Shii grievances and their exploitation by Baghdadian politicians, and on the very nature of Shii opposition to a Sunni dominated state with an official pan-Arab national doctrine. Professor Kedourie explained why Kurds, Shiis, Yazidis and Turkmen were against the intention 'to make Iraq into a great Middle Eastern military power', and why 'Mesopotamia always required strong men to rule over it'.

In the acuteness of their analysis, these studies differed radically from other attempts at explanation given *ipso facto*. Different stages of Iraqi history were described within the framework of their time, without any attempt to fit in the historiographic trends of the moment. They also proved that the history of Iraq's formative years could not account for the emulation of a political platform, nor be tantamount to the narration of a fairy tale.

Professor Kedourie's penetrating views, perspicacious analysis and trenchant style made his students feel that, under his guidance, one would have to deal with 'real people' whose merits and shortcomings were evident, and focus on demystified accounts of their deeds and actions. Under his guidance, historic accounts were to be 'reduced' to their real dimensions, and not inflated artificially by romantic or political interpretations whose veracity is impossible to ascertain. What counted was the real, the palpable, and the human, and their interweaving in shaping the historical event.

Although trained in other systems of inquiry and methodology, I felt ready to engage in a new and fascinating adventure that would bring me closer to understanding Iraq's real problems. 'What do you want to focus on?', was Professor Kedourie's first question, opening a full range of choices from the very beginning of our work together. The sense of liberty he gave, and his respect for the written word (even when it came from a graduate student), remained a constant during all my years of research under his guidance. Professor Kedourie's intervention was sometimes limited to a line, an observation, added in his tiny handwriting at the edge of a page, that would open a whole new spectrum of insights and interpretations. 'What do you mean by ... ?', was a question that often arose, forcing me to reconsider not just the terminology used to define a socio-political development, but the identity of individuals involved therein.

The impact of this kind of inquiry was enormous. It induced me to re-evaluate inculcated ideas, built-in concepts and foregone conclusions. The effect was, at first, one of 'destruction', of dismembered equations and demolished certitudes. 'Did they really exist?' was another question that demolished a long-held assumption regarding the political role played by craftsmen guilds in the weaving of Iraq's social fabric. Other questions followed, making me feel, at the outset, somewhat lost and disoriented. 'The solutions are in the files', was Professor Kedourie's invariable response when approached in one of these moments of despair. It would take some time, months of research, of digging in the infinite number of documents, and in some cases years of reflection, to realize what the right answer was to this and other questions. I gradually realized how constructive his criticism was; it provided a firmer base of facts on which to build. The sources, i.e. the materials to be used, were to be read with care, to be compiled and analysed further within their proper context. Here again, I would sometimes feel discouraged. The sources were numerous, and their meanings in some cases contradictory.

Together with the ability to read 'in between the lines', one also needed to find the correct connections, the invisible ties and the tacit bonds linking one document to another. Here again, Professor Kedourie would come to my aid not just by hinting at the links that seemed, at first sight, non-existent, but also by compelling me to search further and to discover, with great relief, the missing bond, the right piece in the historical puzzle.

The satisfaction, in cases such as this, was great. In other cases, however, the solutions seemed impossible to reach. It was not just the extension of the process, but the requirement of an almost 'intimate' acquaintance with the documents and their authors. In this case, the process of reconstruction could easily be reduced to a mere browsing of files, and to the exposure of their contents, without trying to find the links, between 'causes and effects'. The search for the real meaning of causality was the next step in the debate. Was the relation between 'causes and effects' the sum of explainable or unexplainable reasons, or was it a result of usage, of 'the way they need to be'? Should one opt for the formula 'cause and explanation' rather than the most deterministic one of 'cause and effect'? Cause and explanation emerged then as a better formula to be used as it implies, among other things, the validation of diversity.

'How do we account for diversity?', was obviously the question that followed. In my case, by telling the story of Iraq's inception while underlining the specific, the particular, without totally undermining the generic. How to find the right path between the 'narrow focused' philological analysis of texts, and the broader questions raised by the 'sweeping' inter-disciplinary enquiry? Here again, Professor Kedourie would help me avoid the pitfalls of too specific, or too general, conclusions. 'Iraq is not Egypt', I can still hear him saying. 'You cannot blindly apply in your study of Iraq what you know (or do *not* know) from your previous readings on, say, Egypt.' I was then invited to re-read the texts, to reinsert them in the specific historical and geographical context, and to venture again into more accurate definitions.

Without yet discerning all the facts and implications of the 'history versus social science' debate, I was then taught not to squeeze thoughts into attractive sets of assumptions, nor succumb to theoretical over-simplifications. Each case was a case in point. Hypotheses were to be tested against evidence and presuppositions detailed by date, not the other way around. I also learned how to deal with different sets of values and let myself be impressed and even moved by the richness of cultural diversity. How could culture, in its broader sense, assist in the identification of groups in a society? What was its role in fostering social cohesion? And would a better definition of it help in understanding the 'cultural phenomenon' itself? Caught in the dilemma I would go back to the files and try to find some answers to my preliminary thoughts regarding the display of evidence at my disposal.

Only then would I dare to raise the point again, hoping to receive Professor Kedourie's 'definitive answer'. 'Definite answers' would never come, as I discovered later. 'There is and there isn't' was in most cases the reply, fostering further research and hinting at the challenge to rediscover, time and again, the varying fluctuations between two extreme assumptions. Definite, as it were, was only the rigidity of the methodology, and the respect for the written evidence.

'How do you know?', was one of the questions that popped back into the debate whenever a controversial point was raised or just mentioned matter-of-factly. This approach not only applied to topics whose centrality to the debate was evident, but also to observations that served rather to illustrate the clarity of a point, or merely to describe the atmosphere at a certain moment. 'How do you know that Nuri al-Said was in a "gloomy mood" when he sought refuge at the Residency?,' Professor Kedourie asked after reading my chapter on the 1936 Sidqi-Sulaiman coup. Nuri al-Said's mood was only officially recognized as 'gloomy' when I managed to 'anchor' it in one of the intelligence reports of the time.

The structures of thought and methodology applied also to questions which became categories of their own due to their wide scope. Notions such as 'society versus population', the power of political discourse, 'civic society' and its variants in different societies were concepts ventilated thoroughly before being applied or reapplied to the debate. Their political weight was reappraised within the context of time and culture. 'Could societies transcend their historical past?', was the next step in the debate. Or were the 'power of history' and the 'burden of tradition' too-heavy legacies, preventing societies, populations or human groups from opening themselves to challenges and modernity.

Was the past the only explanation for the present? The answer again was not a simple one. 'Evolution is not a linear process', Professor Kedourie explained, again bringing to my attention other examples of supposedly linear developments that produced sharp contradictions. 'The burden of history' can only be transcended if the weight of tradition and the past could be understood correctly. Otherwise, men, peoples, communities would forever oscillate between collective alienation and violent assertiveness.

On this note our final encounter concluded. I can still see Professor Kedourie bent over his desk at the end of the long dark corridor, the walls of which were covered with books. The debate was closed. At least for the moment. The curve of his frail shoulders as if accentuated by the weight of this conclusion, he kindly offered me a plastic bag in which to carry my heavy thesis home, unimpressed, it seemed, by my fancy leather briefcase. 'Fancy accessories or elaborate arguments do not impress him', I thought to myself once back in the sunny street, 'only the usefulness of an object, or a thought and its applicability in solving problems.'

I took another glance at the impressive building on Houghton Street, knowing then that I would never forget the questions, the debates and the attempts at explanation that took place at the end of the corridor where the darkness seemed illuminated by Professor Kedourie's courage, integrity and clarity of thought.

NOTE

1. 'Continuity and Change in Modern Iraqi History', *Asian Affairs*, Vol.62 (1975) pp.140–96.

Orientation in the 1960s

MICHAEL SUTTON

Most of Elie Kedourie's postgraduate research students at the London School of Economics and Political Science had interests in the contemporary history of the Middle East. Mine lay elsewhere. Indeed, when I was a postgraduate student at the LSE, it was only at master's level that Kedourie was my supervisor. Nonetheless, this brief personal memoir should not come amiss. A large part of his teaching at the LSE was the teaching of philosophy and the history of ideas. It is fitting to recall this important side of his work. At postgraduate level, it was a teaching carried out partly in the framework of Michael Oakeshott's successful creation, the weekly seminar on the history of ideas and the history of political thought, which ran for a few decades and brought together both students and many of the government department's staff who were interested in political ideas.

What led me to the LSE as a part-time postgraduate student in 1966 was the taught master's programme in the history of political thought which revolved around this weekly seminar. This was in the hope that it would help clarify my confused ideas on the respective roles of history and the so-called social sciences. I was not to be disappointed, and – thanks to an interest in Hegel – it was my good fortune to be allocated Elie Kedourie as supervisor. Mentor in the truest sense, not only did he provide an apprenticeship in academic learning, he also imparted a rich understanding of the nature of knowledge and, in the case of history, of its complex spiritual or idea-laden dimension. Coupled to this was his ability to communicate, soberly and without fanfare, a reasoned and yet compassionate historical view of the large-scale human misery and suffering that has been the political lot of so much of the twentieth century.

His approach to the study of politics was scarcely in keeping with the general spirit of the 1960s. In the subjects of political science and international relations, that decade had been the heyday of behaviouralism in the great North American universities, at least until the near intractable Vietnam War dinted the facile optimism that underlay so much policy-oriented model-building and empirical data-gathering. Recalcitrant to these fashions at the LSE were both the government department, of which Elie Kedourie was such a leading light, and the international relations department, where Martin Wight – whom Kedourie knew well – had taught up to the beginning of the 1960s. Kedourie was not one to harp at length on the radical deficiencies of this sort of social science; he tended rather to ignore it. But, if he was pointedly asked about the behavioural approach, he proved to be knowledgeable as well as incisive in his criticism.

My own itinerary had made me interested in such matters. As an undergraduate I had studied at a decidedly old-fashioned institution; and, on the other hand, prior to going to the LSE, I had imbibed a strong dose of American behavioural political science. The undergraduate home was University College, Dublin. Political economy, political studies and modern history were my chosen undergraduate subjects. In the early 1960s, the political economy department bore the mark of the recently retired George O'Brien, famed for his contribution to the history of medieval economic thought; by contrast, a younger member of the department, concerned with the *hic et nunc* of practical economic affairs, was the future Irish prime minister, Garret FitzGerald. The teaching of political studies was the task of an 'ethics and politics' department, whose very name testified to the lingering vitality of a tradition of Aristotelianism and neo-Thomism largely associated with Louvain. My own degree course immersed me in this tradition of linking politics with ethics, a tradition which at UCD owed something also to Sir Ernest Barker. The history department was strong and richly diverse. Lecturing on the history of political thought was John Morrall, who was to move to the LSE before I arrived there in 1966, while the chair of modern history was held by the redoubtable Desmond Williams.

In October 1947, it may be remarked, Desmond Williams had been one of the founders of *The Cambridge Journal*. Indeed, in the first months of life of this intellectually vigorous monthly review, he had been its general editor. Returning to Dublin in 1949 he was to remain on its editorial board until the review was wound up in 1954. His successor as general editor, from 1948 through to the very end, was Michael Oakeshott. And in the early years of the review Oakeshott contributed to it four of the essays that were later to make up his *Rationalism and Politics*, including the essay which gives that book its title. For the young Elie Kedourie too, *The Cambridge Journal* provided an intellectual home. Thus, in October 1951 it published his reflections on *Dans la bataille de la Méditerranée*, a recently published memoir by General Catroux, who had been General de Gaulle's delegate-general in the Levant from 1941 to 1943. Entitled 'Anglo-French Rivalry in the Levant', this essay was signed by Kedourie under the pseudonym of Antiochus, the protagonist in Racine's *Bérénice* who had spoken of his melancholy as he surveyed the vast Syrian desert. For Kedourie, neither party to the rivalry had taken the measure of Syrian nationalism. In June 1954, under his own name, he contributed a second essay 'Colonel Lawrence' to the monthly review. Today, fifty years after Williams and Oakeshott launched *The Cambridge Journal*, anyone glancing at its contents during its seven-year existence cannot but be struck by the distinction and wide range of interests of its contributors; they made for a broad church, the review never having been the organ of an intolerant school of conservatism.

To speak of myself again, I left Dublin in 1964 marked by the latter-day Aristotelianism of UCD's ethics and politics department, and yet also vaguely dissatisfied with the often intemporal character of this approach. I was, moreover, torn between an interest in what is now termed international political economy and more speculative inquiries. An errant student, I went to Nancy and its Centre Européen Universitaire, whose small teaching staff included Jack Lang, the future minister and confidant of François Mitterrand. It was scarcely an academically serious year. However, the time spent there gave a feel and understanding for France's war-torn past of some twenty years earlier. For the centre's president was François de Menthon. This law professor of aristocratic lineage from the Haute-Savoie had been a major figure in the Resistance (initially in 1940 in the *Liberté* group, which was then a main force in 1941 in the creation of Henri Frenay's wider *Combat* movement). In General de Gaulle's provisional government, he was to be successively justice minister and France's chief prosecutor at Nuremberg; and, as one of the leading figures of the Mouvement Populaire Républicain, he eventually broke with de Gaulle over the question of France's future constitution (with, coincidentally, his opening of France's case at Nuremberg in January 1946 preceding by just three days the decision of de Gaulle to step down from power).

Yale was to be my port of call immediately before the LSE. Enrolled as a graduate student in a near phantom international relations department – the courses being provided interdepartmentally, mostly by the political science and economics departments (the latter a truly excellent one) – I found myself confronted with Karl Deutsch's efforts to apply cybernetics to international relations and to enlighten policy-makers through modular analysis using quantitative indicators held, in principle, in ever more elaborate data bases. It was world removed from a French provincial university town in the early years of the Fifth Republic. Nancy and Dublin were perhaps an improbable preparation for the delights of American political science!

In that academic year of 1965–66 some of us in the Graduate School watched the then escalating conflict in Vietnam with concern and foreboding. Perhaps we were overly in the thrall of a youthful desire to set the world to rights and imbued with an excessive moralism. In any case, this new scientistic 'international relations' appeared of little relevance to America's unfolding tragedy. More to the point, for example, was listening to the public lectures of a Staughton Lynd (the Yale academic and Quaker pacifist who had visited Hanoi in 1965 to the ire of many Americans) or, at the other extreme, a Barry Goldwater (who addressed the Yale Law School on Vietnam not long afterwards). Even from a scholarly standpoint, untutored as our judgement may have been, the replacement of an essentially historical approach to questions of political conflict or international relations by a behavioural one – inspired partly by Max Weber (in respect of the quest for value-free objectivity) and partly by Harold Lasswell (in respect of a reductionist social-science method) – seemed to mark regress in our capacity for understanding. A visit to Yale by Hans Morgenthau, during which he spoke about the war, appeared as a breath of fresh air, almost paradoxically inasmuch as the freshness was that of a more traditional approach.

Especially during this year in America, I keenly felt the need to find my way – philosophically speaking. And it was in the same frame of mind that I went immediately afterwards to the LSE. Thanks to Elie Kedourie and Michael Oakeshott, I came to see more clearly that much of my earlier Dublin education had been sounder than I had sometimes initially thought. Having sought to find a better understanding of society through the social sciences, I returned to the historical approach. In his supervision, Kedourie insisted on the importance not only of the practice of history but also of an understanding of the philosophy of history. Writings of Dilthey, Croce, Collingwood, Whitehead and Oakeshott (*Experience and its Modes* being greatly admired by Kedourie) were all required reading. The academic understanding of politics could only be historical. Indeed the academic understanding of philosophy had at root to be historical too. I benefited like others from Kedourie's intellectual lucidity, a lucidity that was underpinned by his being both a practising historian and a penetrating philosopher.

If asked to specify what I learnt most from Elie Kedourie, I should like to stress two quite different sides of an LSE apprenticeship. First, in his setting subjects for essays dealing with the history of political ideas and in his comments afterwards, he taught that the writing of a competent text was – in the best sense of the term – *artisanal*. Once the first initial probing questions had been asked, coherence and clarity of thought based on evidence was the essence of the enterprise, wherever the dialectic of the inquiry led. Hence the importance of careful and crafted language, which was so much his own hallmark. Shaping a historical text had necessarily a palpable feel. There were no magic shortcuts; painstaking work and respect of the subject matter were what counted.

The second fruit of an apprenticeship under the guiding hand of Elie Kedourie was an understanding of the fundamental importance for the history of political thought of the religious dimension. Any untutored student embarking upon political studies became, of course, soon aware of the importance of the religious dimension for political thought during the

period of medieval Christendom and at the beginning of the modern period.
It was quite another matter to be shown in detail – and here I am recalling
Kedourie's lectures open to undergraduates and postgraduates alike – how,
before the Christian era, religious ideas provided so much of the
underpinning of the concept of the Greek *polis* and how, in the modern
period, the political thought of the Enlightenment and later political thought
in the wake of the French Revolution had frequently a religious dimension,
even if the religion in question was of a surrogate nature. Indeed, for so
many modern political thinkers who refused all established religion or
theistic belief, this (secular) religious dimension to their ideas was often
crucial for any proper understanding of their endeavour. In place of Divine
Providence had come Revolution and Progress.

Elie Kedourie's deep interest in Hegel appeared as an interest that was
both philosophic (in respect of his exploring of Hegel's thought) and
religious (in respect of much of the subject matter). In the richness of
Hegel's thought – for instance, his opposition and reconciliation of
Moralität and *Sittlichkeit* in the *Philosophy of Right* – there is to be found a
wealth of reflections relating to the nature of law, individual conscience and
the hierarchy of man's ends, all of which Kedourie long meditated over. As
a small illustration of his own reading, among the books he recommended
on the subject of the revolution in thought between the Hellenic period and
the Christian era, which plays such a central role in the *Philosophy of Right*,
were Edward Caird's *Hegel*, M. B. Foster's *The Political Philosophies of
Plato and Hegel* and Charles Norris Cochrane's *Christianity and Classical
Culture*, the last-mentioned having also been much admired by W. H.
Auden. On first entering Kedourie's office at the LSE in 1966, I had spied
a large tome on his shelves dealing with the history of eschatology – it was
a far cry from the then fashionable behaviouralism of the social sciences.

At the LSE the religious dimension to Elie Kedourie's interest in Hegel
became (even) more apparent after the 1960s. Then, the *Philosophy of Right*
had been the subject of a seminar class, which, if my memory serves me
well, consisted largely of a paragraph-by-paragraph exegesis of Hegel's
text. However, in the mid-1970s Kedourie started to give an annual series
of introductory lectures on Hegel and Marx. After his death, the manuscript
of these lectures was to be edited by Sylvia and Helen Kedourie and
published in 1995. This book *Hegel and Marx* contains a commentary on
the *Philosophy of Right* which is particularly illuminating on two scores: the
role of civil society in Hegel's political philosophy, and, as regards the
latter, its religious side. There are thus some very fine pages on the religious
ideas of Lessing, Kant, Schiller, Schelling and Hölderlin; they make up
indeed a quarter of the book. In the light of these pages, the account later in
the same book of Feuerbach's reading of Hegel is especially telling. There

is a broad sweep to this work of intellectual history which sets it apart, and I know of nothing comparable in English. However, to look at works in French, there is a certain affinity between Kedourie's approach and that of two books by the late Henri de Lubac – a historian of ideas as well as a most distinguished theologian – namely *Le drame de l'humanisme athée*, which is mentioned in *Hegel and Marx*, and *La postérité spirituelle de Joachim de Flore*.

This brings me to my doctoral thesis on Charles Maurras, positivism and French Catholic thought. It was prepared at the LSE under the competent and helpful supervision of William Pickles, who had been invited into the government department after the Second World War by Harold Laski. Yet the initial idea for the thesis had come from Elie Kedourie, once he had quickly shot down a first proposal of mine, thereby earning another title to gratitude. For I had suggested an abstruse and probably hopeless topic: something to do with Auguste Comte and political romanticism. He smiled that gentle smile of his, knowing and slightly mischievous, and warned me happily off the dreadful and endless prose of the founder of positivism. If you are interested in positivism and French political thought, he said, why not look at one of two far more readable writers, either Alain (Emile Chartier) – who, as a moralist and pacifist, had wielded such an influence on the generation entering the prestigious Ecole Normale Supérieure during the 1920s (the generation of Jean-Paul Sartre and Raymond Aron) – or else the quite different Charles Maurras. After some reflection, it was Maurras I chose. And this led to the discovery of the work of the philosopher, Maurice Blondel, who had been one of the first to criticize Maurras's political Catholicism. Almost a decade later, Elie Kedourie and Maurice Cowling kindly accepted the finished work for publication in their Cambridge University Press series, Cambridge Studies in the History and Theory of Politics.

At the outset of my postgraduate research on Maurras's thought, I had not been especially concerned to determine whether or not his doctrinaire nationalism fitted the analysis of Elie Kedourie's *Nationalism*, a book which remains today, nearly forty years after its first publication, a small masterpiece. The initial focus was rather on exploring the links between Maurras's nationalism and, on the other hand, Auguste Comte's positivism and religion of Humanity. Only as the work progressed did I realize how directly pertinent was Kedourie's treatment of Kant and Fichte to an understanding of the endeavour of both Maurras and Comte.

There was much left unsaid in *Nationalism* which Kedourie drew out in his subsequent writings on the Middle East. An example among many is his occasional comments on the doctrinaire politics and person of Michael Aflaq, one of the founders of the Ba'th Party in Damascus in 1940–41.

More generally, his long introduction to the texts contained in his
Nationalism in Asia and Africa – an introduction that could have been a
book in its own right – and his *Politics in the Middle East* show, in broad
sweep, how doctrinaire nationalism was exported from Europe. There is,
moreover, a great deal that can still be drawn out of what is indicated or
suggested in *Nationalism* in respect of Europe's own past two centuries. For
instance, there is arguably a need to clarify further the nature of Thomas
Masaryk's espousal of Czech nationalism, which, as an intellectual or
existential option, was strikingly similar to Maurras's. For Masaryk too, as
has been shown by Roman Szporluk, was indebted to Auguste Comte, and
his embracing of nationalism had a definitely secular religious quality, with
the idea of nationality being expressly linked by him to the idea of
Humanity.

No person who knew Elie Kedourie even only moderately well could not
but be impressed by his quiet and firm respect for the traditional or orthodox
practice of the three religions of Judaism, Christianity and Islam. In inverse
relation to this respect was his scorn for their perversion by modern political
ideas. Where Christian Churches or Islam became the accomplices of
ideological nationalism, they perverted radically their own faiths. In the
case of modern politics and Judaism, he distinguished clearly between
Zionism and the state of Israel. His knowledge of the history of religions in
the lands around the Mediterranean was profound. His death in 1992
occurred a year before Samuel Huntington published his famous article
'The Clash of Civilizations' in *Foreign Affairs*. It must be a matter of
considerable regret that this influential and justly controversial article,
warning of the cataclysmic effects of supposedly insuperable politico-
religious 'cultural fault lines', could not have been rebutted by Kedourie.
The determinism of Huntington's curious amalgam of American political
science and the taxonomy of civilizations associated with Arnold Toynbee
– for whose speculations Kedourie held little regard – would have been
wisely dismissed.

Let me allow myself a few more reflections of a personal kind. Since
childhood I had had experience of the ideological side of Irish nationalism,
partly through older persons' reminiscences of both the 1919–21 Anglo-
Irish war and the 1922–23 Irish civil war and their acquaintanceship also
with people who had been directly involved. Yet by family convictions and
background (part of it in England) as well as an Irish Jesuit schooling, I
grew up closer in spirit to the Home Rule party of Parnell and Redmond.
The rhetoric and complications of nationalism in nineteenth and twentieth-
century Ireland were anyhow familiar. My reading of Elie Kedourie's
Nationalism did not change my views about Ireland's modern past. But it
added a very instructive additional perspective. For instance, it is only from

Kedourie's sort of historical standpoint that the ideological nationalism of a Patrick Pearse can be properly understood in a European context. From this standpoint, some affinity may be seen between a Pearse and a Maurras, however different their religious susceptibilities and however more vast the Frenchman's culture and intelligence.

Again on the question of Ireland, there is the figure of W. B. Yeats, whose poetry Elie Kedourie loved along with that of T. S. Eliot. As epigraph on the title page of *Nationalism* stand lines from 'Nineteen Hundred and Nineteen'. 'We have pieced our thoughts into philosophy, /And planned to bring the world under rule, /Who are but weasels fighting in a hole.' Furthermore, as has been pointed out before, it is in the universal dimension of another of Yeats's poems, namely 'An Irish Airman foresees his Death', which Kedourie so appreciated, that one finds an echo of his own approach to life. 'My country is Kiltartan Cross, /My countrymen Kiltartan's poor, /No likely end could bring them loss /Or leave them happier than before.' If Kedourie had often in public an austere bearing, and if many of his writings are marked by a conservatism tinged with pessimism, he bore much affection for his fellow men, perhaps especially when they were grouped in 'little platoons' – to use the phrase of another Irishman, Edmund Burke – these being the germ of love of country and humankind. However, through his understanding of the nature of the pursuit of academic knowledge, Kedourie knew his work had little or nothing to do with the prompt bearing of glad tidings. There was no message to shout at Kiltartan Cross.

To conclude by returning to the LSE in the second half of the 1960s, it was reputedly the time of student revolt, now sometimes remembered in a haze of sentimental nostalgia about that decade. However, the student remonstrances in the 1968/69 academic year (the second year of the LSE's 'troubles') – which were remonstrances whose extent and support were exaggerated by the press – seemed to verge almost on pantomine farce. Histrionics in London about American imperialism, not to speak of the other supposed misdeeds of capitalism, were too facile when not patently ignorant. In contrast to the position of several years earlier, the war was far engaged; it would be resolved militarily or by compromise; and the signs in 1968 were already pointing to the latter. An American postgraduate student friend was a Vietnam war veteran preparing a doctoral thesis on Platonic Utopia and the Ideal State in sixteenth-century Renaissance Italy; his rare words about the war to us – my wife having also been a postgraduate student at the LSE – testified to a harsh and complicated world remote from the sound of easily voiced slogans.

How bemused was Elie Kedourie by this student posturing? I cannot speak for him. But Yeats's words might have come to mind. 'The best lack all conviction, while the worst /Are full of passionate intensity.' Certain ethical values had been corroded, a sense of tragedy gone. Kedourie knew well that the climate of ideas in the Britain of the 1960s – largely the climate of the entire post-war period until then – was not one that had fostered a real understanding of either the intractable nature of so much political conflict or the depths of barbarism and evil to which the twentieth century had plunged, most notably in Europe. The staple blend of liberalism and utilitarianism might justify *ex post* long-established values and provide *ex ante* some quite radical new ones. Yet, to borrow once more Yeats's words, it has encouraged a frame of mind in which 'the centre cannot hold'.

If the 'centre' cannot hold, it has been primarily because of modern man's unilateral preoccupation with self. Like no doubt many others who listened at the LSE to Elie Kedourie's commentaries on Hegel's *Philosophy of Right*, I well remember the great attention he paid to the pages in that work containing Hegel's powerful critique of subjectivism and, in particular, of the descent of evil to the stage at which subjectivity claims to be absolute. One pointer to an understanding of Kedourie's own mind is surely the comment in his *Hegel and Marx* that these important pages from the *Philosophy of Right* may be read as 'the drama of the modern European psyche, with its taste for annihilation and self-annihilation'.

Elie Kedourie leaves a rich and diverse legacy; many of us have benefited in a variety of ways from both his great learning and personal kindness. As a spiritual child of the 1960s, I learnt from him the value of philosophically-informed historical scholarship. I learnt too that meaning and hope were in no way incompatible with a truthful appraisal of a very imperfect world.

A Memoir

NOËL O'SULLIVAN

I will always remember my LSE days best for the encounter they brought with three people. They were Michael Oakeshott, Maurice Cranston and Elie Kedourie. Oakeshott was the philosopher (and, more than that, part gentleman, part bounder, part dandy, and part monk). Cranston was the eighteenth-century man of letters (and, over and above that, a would-be Whig grandee on the one hand, and heir to Balzac's highly mobile Rastignac on the other). Kedourie was the scholar *par excellence* (and, what is more, a just and wise man, who saw that the face of God was inscrutable, and that human nature was all but impossible, and yet nevertheless retained a regard for measure, and a desire to establish it in politics, even when the storm raged and there was little or no reason to expect success). He was also, it should be added, a truly pious man – pious, not in the Christian but the classical sense of being free from *hubris*, and able in consequence to acknowledge without rancour those features of the human condition not of our making, and which only folly seeks to bring under the empire of the will. In this sense, the eloquent words used by Santayana apply in full measure to him. Piety, Santayana wrote,

> is never so beautiful and touching, never so thoroughly humane and invincible, as when it is joined to an impartial intellect, conscious of the relativity involved in existence and able to elude, through imaginative sympathy, the limits set to personal life by circumstance and private duty. As a man dies nobly when, awaiting his own extinction, he is interested to the last in what will continue to be in the interests and joys of others, so he is most profoundly pious who loves unreservedly a country, friends, and associations which he knows very well to be not the most beautiful on earth, and who, being wholly content in his personal capacity with his natural condition, does not need to begrudge other things whatever speculative admiration they may truly deserve.

I record here some fragments of a purely personal impression of Elie formed initially as an undergraduate who had him as tutor in my third year, and then as one who turned to him, until his death, for intellectual advice in the various projects in which I later became involved. The fact that I may occasionally happen to strike an irreverent note will not, I trust, obscure the fact that the memoir is inspired by a mixture of gratitude and unqualified esteem.

My first meeting with Elie was at once unusual and amusing. It was unusual, because I was not daunted by Elie, who was generally found to be a very daunting man. But it was also amusing. In order to explain why, I must digress slightly for a moment and say a word, by way of background, about my own experience of the LSE up to the point when I first met him.

It was just before the end of the Christmas term in my third year when I first found my way to the door of Elie's room in the old E wing by taking the slow and creaky wrought iron lift to the second floor. I was in good spirits because the vacation was about to begin and I was intending to get the train home from London the following day. At this point in my undergraduate career, I must add, I had no interest in tutors, and ended up outside Elie's door that day only as a token gesture of courtesy, inspired in part by a desire simply to keep out of trouble with the powers that be. I had in fact long since written off the formal side of LSE teaching as of no possible concern or profit to me, except for Oakeshott's lectures, and some atmospheric tutorials by Cranston I had just started attending. This attitude did not reflect any great intellectual arrogance on my part; it was just that everything that had previously happened to me seemed to have had a hopelessly comic character from which I derived some pleasure, but no intellectual gain. Above all, at this point I was desperately pressed for time, since I was soon to be faced by final examinations in a special subject I had not taken up until the third year.

Most of what had happened during the two and a bit years of my undergraduate life prior to the time I found myself standing outside Elie's door was due to the fact that for much of that time I had been studying for the Accountancy degree, and had gradually resigned myself to accepting that everything and everyone to do with it came either from the Victorian world of Dickens, or the spiv world of finance that the 1960s was beginning to spawn, or the developing world of darkest Africa. My experience of the accountancy degree began with the dark African world when, at the start of my first year, and still fresh from the farm I had left behind in Staffordshire, I was assigned to an African tutor called Mr Olakanpo. He was, I have no doubt, a very brilliant man; but I just could not understand a word he was saying. For example, when he asked me at my first personal tutorial with him to write an essay called, 'Is economics a dismal science?', the only way I could make sense of what he was saying, after asking him to repeat it several times, was to get him to spell it slowly. Obviously, if I was rattled by this, I could see that he in his turn was wondering what the level of literacy was like in that year's intake of students. The Victorian element was embodied in the gentle but austerely aloof and melancholy Professor Baxter, who gave us a set of company accounts if we had been good and done our accountancy homework exercises neatly (alas, I was never deemed worthy of a set), and whose eyes only ever sparkled as he sometimes recounted to us the ingenuity that had gone into some of the biggest frauds that the European financial world had experienced. The spiv element was something I only encountered at first hand in the second year, when an Australian tutor replaced my African one. The Australian sat with his feet on his desk at our first meeting and said, 'Whatever else happens, don't forget to remind me to take that parcel home with me – it has my underpants in it.' I trust that he remembered.

After two years of the accountancy tutors, I saw at length that I was no good at the subject, and changed to the Government Department for my final year, having mentally convinced myself by this stage, as I said, that the tutoring world at the LSE was not made for the likes of me, and having also decided that my late change of plans inevitably meant that any tutor I was assigned to would be someone to whom my new department passed its weakest children, amongst whom I thought I probably occupied pride of place. So I am afraid to say that, in the mind of the nineteen-year-old who stood outside Elie's door, this particular relationship had been well and truly written off before it even began.

As I stood there in the silent corridor I could hear Elie through the door: he was severely castigating a student who had obviously done an appalling term's work. Then the door opened, the cowed student sloped past me, and it was my turn. Elie was still angry. He glared at me and said, 'Why haven't I heard from you before?' At this I immediately began to feel mildly indignant and irritated – remember, I thought of myself as only being there at all from indulgent and courteous instincts that were obviously not being appreciated as much as I had expected them to be – and replied, 'I am here because I was wondering why I have not heard from you, either,' at which there was a sort of stalemate, and he invited me into what was no more than a tiny cubby-hole. I remember it vividly because I was a heavy pipe smoker in those days, and Elie never complained when I made the room uninhabitable every time I went to see him by lighting up the dreadful St Bruno flake I used to smoke (in homage to one of my Irish grandfathers) in those days.

Anyway, he asked me to do an essay. I took him aback by saying that I was afraid I could not do that for him. He naturally looked both surprised and grim, but managed to ask me politely why not. I explained that I had been doing the Accountancy degree and now only had a few months left of the third year to do the Government degree, and had devised my own personal programme and schedule, and could only accommodate work that fitted in with it. He immediately accepted this, and we got on well after that. He asked me about my programme, and we fixed some essays in line with it, and he also recommended a few things to read. I think that what won me round more effectively, though, was that he let me borrow a volume from Burke's collected works that was in his bookcase, and I appreciated this as a mark of personal confidence. That, and the fact that he did not play about with ideas, or try to impress me by learned references, but spoke directly and simply, and took it for granted that some ideas and some academics were up the creek, were the things that impressed me. There was, however, something else that also struck me vividly at that first encounter.

This was that from his wonted expression of profound seriousness and gravity, Elie could pass in a flash into a deep laughter that shook his whole being. For example, when he was asking me about my programme at that first meeting, I said I found comparative politics very difficult because I did not understand the terms being used in the books, and could not find them in the dictionary. He asked for an example, and I said that I had been reading a book by Almond and Coleman which described a riot as an anomic expression of interest articulation. He immediately shook with laughter, and the atmosphere changed, and I remember him saying that what this meant was that they could not tell the difference between a riot in London and a riot in Bangkok.

After I graduated, I was in the United States for a time. Whilst there I studied with Eric Voegelin, whose interest was in what he considered to be the spread in western modernity of a highly destructive secular version of the ancient Gnostic heresy. When I got back I discovered that Voegelin had recently given a public lecture at the School on the Gnostic roots of the modern ideological consciousness, but that no-one who had attended it seemed to have a clue about what he meant. The odd man out was Elie, with whom I discussed the Gnostic vision one evening as we walked to Holborn. He summed it up accurately and neatly, as usual, in two images. For the Gnostic, he said, life is a prison or, as the more familiar way of thinking would have it, a condition of alienation. It is, secondly, a condition from which escape is possible, in the form of liberation brought about by a special form of knowledge (or gnosis). In the space of a few minutes, Elie would have made the nature of modern gnosticism clearer to an audience than Voegelin had managed to do in an hour.

It was not long afterwards that I visited him in a Hampstead hospital, as soon as I heard about his heart attack. He was lying back eating water-cress, with a massive tome in Arabic balanced, open, on his chest. He had no small talk and I was obviously distracting him from the Arabic work in which he had been absorbed, so the time I was there was mainly spent in mutual silent meditation. When I got back to the School, I bumped into Oakeshott, who was worried about Elie's consuming propensity for overwork. I asked if there was any remedy and Oakeshott said yes, there was one. I asked him what it was, and he said: a dog. Elie would have to be presented with a dog, so that he would have to break off to take it for walks on Hampstead Heath.

When he recovered I saw him weekly at Oakeshott's seminar on the history of political thought, which he invariably attended. He generally chaired it, and when he did so he sat by Oakeshott in a slightly hunched sideways position that gave the impression of a highly protective samurai guarding his vulnerable and incautious master from the rabble to which the master was for the moment being exposed. Elie rarely spoke, but when he did, what he said was usually memorable for its gnomic, and sometimes epigrammatic, character. It was, at any rate, always very brief and striking. I remember several instances, all of which either created a totally baffled silence amongst those present, or else led everyone to dissolve in a gale of laughter. So far as the latter, gale-of-laughter effect goes, I remember the subject of Nazi extermination policy coming up and someone saying, in all good faith, 'But suppose you did have a Jewish problem?' At which Elie suddenly leaned forward with great interest and attention, and said: 'Yes – what would you do? Please do go on.' As I say, there was a roar of laughter. There was also one when an American postgraduate who was giving a paper started apologizing to those present because, he said, he was coming to a very difficult and intellectual bit. Elie leaned forward again on this occasion and asked him not to worry, telling him that he was in fact in an extremely intellectual place. As for the silences: someone would advance a thought for consideration, and Elie would say that this was exactly the kind of thing you might hear on television any night of the week; or, on another occasion, that it was the kind of thing we could have learned just by looking out of the window at the clouds. As I say, a puzzled silence would follow.

At those seminars, I often reflected on the relationship between Elie and Michael. Elie gave me the impression, through the protective manner he had towards Michael, that should the need arise he would fight for him like a tigress for her young. Michael, in his turn, greatly respected Elie's judgement, and I once remember deliberately irritating him mildly by exploiting this fact. It was after *On Human Conduct* came out in 1975. I was talking to Oakeshott about the different critical reactions, and asked him whether he knew Elie's response. Oakeshott said no, and I kept silent, to see if his curiosity would get the better of him and compel him to ask me. It did. He looked at me half sheepishly, and half in irritation, and said abruptly, 'What did he say?' I am quite certain that Elie was the only living person in whose opinion Oakeshott would have shown that interest, and about whose view he would have permitted himself to ask me that question. I replied that Elie had told me he was delighted by the book, but found it so demanding that he had to read it backwards. Oakeshott said nothing but looked quite pleased. There is one other thing I remember Elie saying about Oakeshott. We were discussing Oakeshott's philosophy in general, and I said that an unusual feature was the absence of any sense of bitterness or *ressentiment*.

Elie nodded his head thoughtfully and said approvingly, 'Yes, he is gentle.'

I was not at Elie's own seminars too often, but did attend his Hegel course one year in which I prompted (it didn't take much doing) Shirley Letwin and Ken Minogue to sit in as well. I remember the atmosphere, which was rather like a weekly Bible-reading session. A few passages from the *Philosophy of Right* would be read out by a student who had been assigned the task of reflecting on and introducing them, and questions would be strictly confined to those passages. The result was that there was mostly silence, since we all feared that our comments would appear fanciful, irrelevant, or simply ill-informed. I am afraid this was the kind of occasion on which I taxed Elie's patience sorely, since I had an overwhelming urge to open up the discussion by getting onto the nature of God, immortality, and the essence of the human condition before the hour was out. He took a stern line on wayward tendencies like that, but I remember well how kind and gentle, and deeply concerned, he became when one or two of the students who had to give an introductory talk showed signs of strain or stress. He would lean forward and speak to them very quietly, asking them not to worry.

I myself once experienced this extreme concern and kindness in a way that meant much to me. After I returned from an interview for a lectureship that I failed in the event to secure, Elie invited me into his room and questioned me about what had happened. Then he gazed at me intensely, asked me not to be down-hearted, and told me to use his name whenever I thought it might help me. Years later I saw the same kindness once more, when I was invited to be external examiner for a thesis on the nature of the history of political thought which he had supervised. Sounding me out over lunch (I recollect being more nervous than the student must have been) to see that everything was all right, he looked relieved and pleased when I said that I thought the student was very brave to have taken the subject on at all. He nodded in firm agreement, and simply added that he was even more impressed by the fact that the student had actually managed to finish a thesis on such a potentially shapeless topic.

He was not merely a wise, just and gentle man, however. He was also a deeply passionate one. This sometimes came through very powerfully in his writing, as for example in his famous castigation of Lawrence of Arabia in his first book. The chapter in which this occurred had so arrested Oakeshott that he published it as an article in the *Cambridge Journal*. Usually, however, the depth of his passion was most evident in conversations which hinted at the range of literature to which an imagination born of educated passion had given him access. I think particularly of his esteem for Montherlant's *The Master of Santiago*, in which passion blends with a sort of detached charity to yield a mix in which sanctity and nihilism come dangerously close to union. I remember, in the same connection, mentioning Montherlant's early novel on bull-fighting, to which Elie replied by asking me whether I knew that the novel was autobiographical, and added that Montherlant had taught himself bull-fighting against his parents' express wishes. I recalled that after he lost half of his stomach as a result of being gored, Montherlant decided to devote the rest of his life to pursuing happiness. Montherlant himself records that for eight years he was completely successful in this pursuit, but then abandoned it out of sheer boredom, and devoted the rest of his life to writing. Elie gave one of his great laughs and said he had just seen a Montherlant play in Paris – it was, I think, *The Civil War.*

The same passion was reflected in his taste in political literature. I have in mind in particular his admiration for de Maistre. In the ordinary way, such a thinker would be tagged (like Montherlant) with the reactionary label, and thereafter comfortably ignored. But what Elie saw there was more than the surface politics: it was the underlying vision of existence, capable in the end only of poetic and religious expression, and most fully and inspiringly conveyed in the *St. Petersburg Dialogues.* There, in that vision of the fiery furnace of existence in which all things human are at once forged and, in the very process of being forged, are simultaneously incinerated – a vision that lies beyond the moral and the ethical, and sets the political idealism of Western humanism at nought – I think he found the vantage point from which he thought and wrote, and lived.

So far as politics are concerned, there was at the heart of Elie's thought a tension of which I only became fully conscious many years after I had graduated. If that tension remained unresolved, that is only because it is the irresoluble tension on which our political world itself is based. This is the tension between good government and self-government. In a report for the publisher of his posthumous volume of lectures on *Hegel and Marx* that I wrote after Elie's death, I tried to pinpoint the bearing of that tension upon his political thought in the following words:

> In his well-known studies of the theory and practice of nationalism, Kedourie provided a profound exploration of one of the most important aspects of that tension. The present volume contains his lectures on a second manifestation of it, which is Marxism. Kedourie's reflections on Marx, made available here for the first time, are the fruit of a unique blend of philosophical and historical scholarship that makes what he has to say indispensable reading not only for students of the history of political thought but also for anyone concerned to understand the continuing sources of political instability and extremism in the Western world.

Marx, of course, wrote in the shadow of Hegel. In Hegel's thought Kedourie rightly found the most ambitious attempt to stabilize modern Western political life by a synthesis that reconciled the two potentially conflicting ideals of self-government and good government. In particular, Kedourie saw prefigured in the difficulties posed by Hegel's attempted synthesis, and in the powerful critique of it mounted by Marx, the problem that has remained central to the survival of Western liberal democracy down to the present day. This is the problem of combining the classical liberal ideal of civil society (along with the related ideal of limited politics) with the broader hope of finding in modern social and political life a sense of justice and a form of ultimate meaning that would console men for the coldness of a disenchanted secular existence. In the clear, masterly prose that characterized everything he wrote, Kedourie's posthumously published lectures weigh the difficulties presented by such a synthesis.

Unfortunately, Kedourie did not live to elaborate his lectures into the complete, fully polished expression of his thought for which those already indebted to him had been waiting. Nevertheless, the sustained philosophical rigour, range of imaginative sympathy, and depth of historical insight, displayed in his reflections on Hegel's proposed synthesis and Marx's critique of it ensure that this volume will confirm his status as one the greatest political thinkers to have emerged during the second half of the twentieth century.

I last saw Elie a year or two before he died. It was at a fairly small Liberty Trust conference on Oakeshott, and we spent one evening together over dinner. We talked of many things, including the fortunes of those he remembered from my own generation who were teaching in British and American universities. I asked if he knew that an American doctoral student who had attended some of the Oakeshott seminars had managed as a side line to have a play on the Holocaust produced on BBC TV while he was here. Elie reflected for a moment and said, 'I thought everything he did was on the side.' He also asked me for word of two of my contemporaries in the LSE postgraduate school who had, like myself, gone on to teach in British universities, and it was clear that he had followed the dramatic fall of one, and the spectacular rise of the other telly-stardom, with interest. I told him what I knew, and was never certain at the end of such conversations whether the upshot was that he found human beings more or less strange creatures than he had thought them to be.

What I remember best about that evening, however, is his sadness over the state of the universities. He questioned me in some detail about what had happened at Hull, where he knew that William Taylor had won a knighthood by putting through a managerial revolution. Then he told me of his own unhappiness about what was happening at the LSE, where he was clearly out of sympathy with the direction in which the School was moving. He said that he had now chosen all that was left, which he said was 'the inner exile'. I tried to strike a more cheerful note by saying that I thought the mood might well change with economic recovery and more prosperity, since that led people to be more concerned with the wider, more liberal ideal of education which they were presently content to ignore. He agreed that this might indeed happen, but added that it would be too late to undo the permanent harm that had been done. I returned to Hull with his remarks about the inner exile on my mind, pondering the thought that for all his wisdom and knowledge of men and the world he had managed to retain an idealism that amounted, perhaps, to a faith.

Remembering Elie Kedourie in the United States

JOSEPH SHATTAN

I think the first time I came across Elie Kedourie's name was in Saul Bellow's 1976 memoir, *To Jerusalem and Back*. 'Kedourie says nothing off the top of his head,' Bellow wrote. 'His judgments are thoroughly considered. And he is not optimistic.' Elie was especially pessimistic about prospects for resolving the Arab–Israeli dispute, and because I was then a graduate student with a strong interest in Arab–Israeli affairs, Bellow's brief summary of Elie's views left quite an impression on me.

The graduate school I attended, the Fletcher School of Law and Diplomacy, has a well-deserved reputation for training American Foreign Service officers, but I had no intention of joining the Foreign Service. After all, I reasoned, State Department officials must often find themselves in the uncomfortable position of having to defend or implement policies with which they passionately disagree, and while I could certainly sympathize with the need for a foreign service that placed 'professionalism' above conscience, this was not the career I envisaged for myself.

Thus, after obtaining my doctorate at Fletcher, I eventually made my way to Washington and joined UN Ambassador Jeane Kirkpatrick's staff as a 'political' appointee. This enabled me to write speeches for Kirkpatrick, and subsequently for other cabinet-level officials, during the Reagan Administration, and to become Vice President Quayle's principal speechwriter during the Bush Administration. And it was during my tenure with the Vice President that I finally had the opportunity, and the privilege, of meeting Elie Kedourie.

I owe it all, I suppose, to Saddam Hussein. Had he not invaded Kuwait in 1990, I would not have been assigned the task of preparing a speech for the Vice President justifying US policy in the Gulf, and so probably would never have worked up the nerve to contact Professor Kedourie, who was then a Visiting Fellow at the Washington Institute for Near East Policy, and of whose reputation as one of the world's foremost Middle Eastern scholars I was fully aware.

But Saddam did invade Kuwait, and as the United States set about reversing his gains, somebody had to convince the American people that it was vital that we do so. Unfortunately, the task proved too difficult for President Bush, who argued that United States policy was simply an altruistic effort to uphold international law, or for Secretary of State Baker, who explained that we had to act in order to keep the price of oil down. Neither argument was convincing: the notion that a half-million American troops were being sent half way around the world simply out of a disinterested concern for international law seemed preposterous on the face of it, while the prospect that American troops might be ordered to kill or be killed merely to prevent the price of gas from going up a few cents struck many Americans as morally repugnant. To complicate matters further, the National Conference of Catholic Bishops had issued a statement denouncing US policy as likely to lead the country into an unnecessary war, while many on the far right of the Republican Party joined virtually the entire Democratic Party in urging the Administration to keep American troops out of harm's way.

It was within this political context that Quayle's Chief of Staff, Bill Kristol, told me that the Vice President had agreed to deliver a major address on US Gulf policy at Seton Hall University, and asked me to write it. Our conversation, as usual, was quite brief. Kristol, who was never lacking in self-confidence, probably assumed that between the two of us we could easily come up with something far more sensible than what the President and Secretary of State were saying.

But what? It was while pondering this question that I received an invitation to a luncheon and lecture sponsored by a prominent think tank, the Washington Institute for Near East Policy. The topic was 'US Strategic Objectives in the Persian Gulf', and the scheduled speaker was Professor Elie Kedourie. Needless to say, I immediately called the Washington Institute and told them I'd be there.

The day Elie spoke, I arrived at the Washington Institute quite early. Taking a paper plate, I piled it high with some of the goodies that the Institute had thoughtfully spread out across a long buffet table, then seated myself next to an interesting-looking lady who turned out to be Mrs Sylvia Kedourie. We began to chat, and she readily agreed to introduce me to her husband at the conclusion of his remarks.

Although Elie's lecture took place nearly seven years ago, I remember it quite well, both because I took copious notes at the time and – more importantly – because it subsequently became the core of Vice President Quayle's Seton Hall speech. Basically, Elie discussed three traditional American objectives in the Gulf: to contain Soviet expansionism, to prevent any local Middle Eastern power from dominating its neighbors, and to secure an uninterrupted supply of oil at a reasonable price. With the end of the Cold War, the first objective had been realized, but the other two remained as urgent as ever. The Bush Administration, Elie demonstrated, was simply pursuing traditional American objectives in the face of a new and dangerous challenge: Saddam Hussein's attempt to dominate the Gulf.

All this seems perfectly obvious in retrospect, but at the time it constituted something of a revelation. The fact of the matter is that before Vice President Quayle's Seton Hall address, no one in the government had attempted to place our Gulf policy in a wider strategic and moral perspective. And the only reason the Vice President did so is because I took careful notes during Elie's presentation at the Washington Institute.

Although Vice Presidential speeches ordinarily receive little if any attention, on 30 November 1990, Quayle's Seton Hall speech made the front page of the *Washington Post*. According to the *Post*'s Ann Devroy, it 'represented the most systematic attempt of any Administration official, including President Bush, to lay out the historical, political and moral arguments for US policy in the Gulf.' Ms Devroy, whom I have never met but who was generally not considered friendly to the Bush Administration, actually called me up one day out of the blue, told me she had learned that I was the person who had written the Vice President's speech, and wished only to say that in all her years in Washington she had heard many speeches, but few as good as mine.

Within the Administration, the reaction to the speech was also very positive. I particularly remember a note from the National Security Council's top Middle Eastern specialist, Richard Haas, who said that his only reservation about the text was that he had not written it himself. Vice President Quayle was also delighted with the speech. In his memoir, *Standing Firm*, he called it 'the most important speech of my four years as Vice President,' and it was reprinted in the appendix to the book. The speech was also reprinted in the *Washington Post* and discussed widely on national television. Some of its themes eventually found their way into the President's remarks.

The day after Vice President Quayle delivered the speech, I sent a copy to Professor Kedourie, along with a note thanking him for his contribution to it. We subsequently became friends, and had dinner together several times. On one such occasion, I asked Elie if there were any novels he might recommend that conveyed something of the spirit and texture of Middle Eastern life. He came up with three books: *Maze of Justice* by Tawfiq al-Hakim, *Farewell Babylon* by Naim Kattan, and *Three Months on Gaza Street* by Hilary Mantel. I managed to get hold of the first two books, but eventually had to inform Elie that even the US Library of Congress lacked a copy of Mantel's novel. He was astonished.

As I came to know him better, I was often struck by the way Elie combined tremendous intellectual authority with personal modesty, and even shyness. He reminded me of Alexis de Tocqueville, who confessed in his *Recollections* that 'by nature I am full of self-distrust', and who claimed that the one benefit he derived from his brief stint as France's Foreign Minister was 'confidence in myself'. I could not say whether Elie was also filled with 'self-distrust', but he certainly was not overly assertive. At a time when a host of Middle East specialists of dubious expertise were desperately scrambling to get on national television, Elie, who actually had a great deal to offer, never pushed himself forward. Once, after Saddam Hussein's defeat, I asked him whether any government officials besides me had ever approached him during the crisis. He told me that apart from a phone call from a highly placed friend of his in the Defense Department, no one had sought him out.

There were many questions that I had hoped to ask Elie – about the Middle East, of course, but also about things in general – but one awful morning I read in the *Washington Post* that he had died of a sudden heart attack. To this day, I cannot shake off the feeling that he and I were in the midst of a delightful conversation that was rudely – and most unfairly – interrupted. One of the obituaries I came across (written, I believe, by the late Maurice Cranston) pointed out that Elie was an observant Jew, so I suppose it is possible that he and I will be resuming our conversation in heaven – assuming that is where I am headed. In any event, I consider Elie Kedourie to have been a great man, and am grateful for the opportunity to have known him and, thanks to him, to have played what I naturally regard as an important role in the formulation of United States foreign policy at a key juncture in our post-Cold War history.

A Bulwark against Mediocrity

LOUISE GREENBERG

I always joked that I was Elie Kedourie's unmatriculated student for whom he was unremunerated. He would chuckle when I offered this apology. As my husband says, he was a man with an unstinting generosity of knowledge.

Between 1982 and 1990, I produced some half dozen scripted talks and conversations with Elie. Once I got to know him, however, I sought his advice in connection with a great many other programmes. I also had the good luck to live a few steps away from Elie and Sylvia, and was often invited to visit them. I used to wait for the moment, usually over dessert, when one or another of a dozen guests would ask Elie to clarify some issue or event of the day. The calibre of discussion was my private model of the standard for which Radio Three programmes should aim.

I 'inherited' Elie from a producer who had retired and who, unlike me, was English and Oxbridge educated. I already knew of Elie by reputation, of course, and not for the first time as a producer of Radio Three interval talks, felt dismayed by the gap between my own knowledge and that of the person I was going to produce. Eventually, despite his gravitas, I had the privilege of friendship from Elie though I never imagined myself to be in equality with him. He must have been exercising patience with me much of the time but it never showed. I always hoped I was no worse than the majority of his undergraduates. I once asked him, 'Is it possible for an observant Moslem to wear his religion lightly?' I have not forgotten what he told me; it took him a good few minutes just to deal with the ignorance which lay behind the question! I often think of his reply now, when there is news coverage of the demand for state Islamic schools in Great Britain, for instance.

I often tried out my ideas on Elie, not to test myself, and certainly not in the hope of having my thoughts endorsed by a mind I revered, but because of the responsibility of working in a public service medium. I did not mind if Elie knew my ignorance, as long as my programmes were saved from it before they got on the air.

Working far more rapidly than a scholar does, across a variety of fields, it is often possible for a producer to sense that he is on the wrong track without having the time or temperament to correct himself by reading widely. What is more, even the best read, best informed producer cannot gather the intelligence that someone like Elie could, who was constantly advising ministers and heads of government. I went to Elie to find out what was going on, *and* to have myself and my colleagues set straight.

When George Fischer, himself a considerable political mind, and at that time Head of Talks and Documentaries for BBC Radio, wanted to approach Begin about an interview after he had left office, I turned to Elie for advice. We had been trying to think who we knew, or could meet, who could effect an introduction. Elie told me to ask for an appointment with Avner, who was then Israel Ambassador in London. Begin was too unwell to record by that time but the exchange of letters took place under Avner's aegis.

When Michael Charlton was preparing his series about the tensions between the National Security Advisor and the Secretary of State which led to the Iran Contra affair, I thought, as I often did, I had better just ring Elie and tell him what Michael was working on. Elie said, 'Tell Michael, if he will come to my home, he may read the paper I wrote for Mrs Thatcher about whether the Prime Minister should have a security adviser. It wouldn't be proper for me to let it circulate.' Off Michael went, with me breathing a sigh of relief that I had 'bothered' Elie. Anyone who heard Charlton talking to Lord Armstrong about 'the hole in the centre of cabinet government' owed a debt to Elie, without knowing it.

Sometimes, I simply needed to reassure myself about the obvious. When Ian MacDougal, the BBC's Middle East correspondent, by then retired, was preparing talks called *Aspects of Egypt* for Radio Three in 1989, he said, really just thinking aloud, 'There isn't any possibility that Syria would invade Lebanon is there?' I replied, 'Hmmmm. I'll call Elie ...' 'And *why* wasn't there any possibility Syria would invade ... ?' 'Because there are American warships sitting off the coast ...'

Elie was kind enough to listen to a series Michael Charlton and I made about the United Nations as a peace-keeping force. There were three interviews; Waldheim (at that time there were still only rumours about his conduct during the Second World War); Brian Urquhart (who knows the details of the negotiations for every conflict from Indonesia to the invasion of Lebanon) and Conor Cruise O'Brien, the only man who knew by whose authority UN troops were deployed against the Katanga rebels in 1963. Because Dr O'Brien was good enough to take part, Elie considered that we had filled a gap in the historical record.

Michael Charlton said this about Elie, 'I found, as everyone does, I imagine, his scholarship deeply impressive. On the other hand, as an admirer, on the whole, of British statecraft, for which I believe the civilized world has much to be thankful, I did not care overmuch for his *The Chatham House Version and Other Essays*. However, his was a rigorous intellect of the kind which was instructive for the slapdash mind of the broadcaster. I have some of his books on my shelves and I always try to look at them before leaping!' Elie respected Michael because of the thoroughness of

Michael's preparation for an interview he conducted with Elie in 1985 on the occasion of the re-issue of *The Chatham House Version*. Elie said to me afterwards, 'I think he's read everything I've ever written.' I agonized a long time over the title for that programme. It was called, 'The Facts of History' to convey that when Elie uttered, there was no response to make except to digest and retain. I often used to say that his public lectures were not history but prophecy.

After producing the first talk with Elie, I decided to tackle the very occasional misplaced stress which would appear when he was working from a script. It had once been said inside Broadcasting House – as it would be of any foreigner – that he was 'not God's gift to broadcasting'. I had his draft typed up (this was before the computer era) and went along to his house. He read it very well and there were no mistakes to correct. I apologized, 'I needn't have asked you to rehearse!' 'It was easier to see, it's been triple-spaced.' From then on, everything was triple-spaced.

I am aware of committing only one really enormous howler in Elie's presence. (There were probably dozens of others.) I used 'liberal' and 'libertarian' carelessly, over the phone one day. Elie did not say anything at the time but a day later I received in the post, an offprint of his article from *The American Scholar* about the fallacies of Liberal politics. It was not a rebuke, just good teaching. It gave me a good laugh (at myself!).

Of course, Elie did not do the work for one. When I was preparing a series for Radio Four about the social, educational and economic opportunities open to people of African ancestry in Britain, I consulted him about youth training schemes. As usual, I was in a hurry so I rang him, but apologetically. The reply was, 'Review the history of the poor laws!' Ashamed that I could not immediately make the connection, I consulted half a dozen textbooks in the library. 'And when you make the programmes, don't talk about inner cities.'

Occasionally, some of Elie's remarks have been described as cryptic. Perhaps, they could more accurately be called shocking. He said more than once, 'The Shah wasn't ruthless enough!' Not cryptic but painful. Michael Charlton, in 'The Facts of History', pressing Elie to defend his critique of the doctrine of nationalism said, 'Take Yugoslavia ... There are several ... antipathies which coexist, albeit uneasily, at present. Why is the notion of an autonomous Arab state ... doomed to be elusive in the Middle East?' More of us can answer that now.

Among those who did understand his work well, not least with regard to the former Yugoslavia, was Professor Robert Wistrich, who recently gave some talks on Radio Three. Wistrich argues that even the educated elite in Britain, including the Foreign Office, still do not understand, any more than they did in 1914, the multi-confessional, democratic nature of Austro-

Hungary, which was wrongly regarded as nothing but a prison house, and which should not have been broken into its supposedly constituent nationalities. I mentioned Elie's work to him and he said, 'Of course, I agree with him. The only difference between us with regard to the doctrine of nationalism is that I would make an exception for Zionism and Elie would not.' Indeed, another regular contributor to Radio Three whom I had often urged to read Elie's books, rang me a few month's after his death. 'I've finally been reading Elie Kedourie,' he said, 'and I have a question. Tell me, was he a Zionist?' 'No,' I said. And I remember thinking when I saw some of Elie's obituaries that he should not have been represented as a Conservative, either. To consult Elie should not have been to mistake him for a member of your faction.

Rereading Elie's programmes, I was struck by this introductory phrase from 'Religion Under Stress': 'A new ideal of moral autonomy for the individual, irreconcilable with the authority of divine prescription, has become increasingly attractive.' How many attempts to capture the contemporary cast of mind have been made since, without being as succinct!

When Elie suddenly died, I felt that his family's grief, and everyone else's, was intensified by the loss to scholarship and policy. I will end with a note about Elie from George Fischer, who had to produce the actual recording of 'The Facts of History' because I was taken into hospital, briefly, on the day. 'Professor Kedourie's broadcasts were invariably occasions when the listeners could count on original thought and fresh insights. But his immense erudition and intellectual authority were in sharp contrast with his persona. There was a modest, unfailingly courteous man who plainly did not relish the paraphernalia of a studio. He received our praise of his talks and discussion programmes with mild embarrassment and, I think, disbelief. His contributions to cultural broadcasting are of lasting value.'

Memories of a Friendship

ANDREW MANGO

'They are talking of Saddam Hussein's Republican Guard as if they were Prussian Grenadiers,' Elie Kedourie said with a chuckle. We were having a long telephone conversation on the eve of the collapse of the Iraqi army in the Gulf War in February 1991, and sharing our mutual exasperation at the hours of largely worthless analysis and commentary which filled British television screens after Saddam Hussein's occupation of Kuwait. A phrase which occurred frequently, as presenters moved counters across studio maps, was 'the élite Republican Guard', with the word 'élite' emphasized to suggest a formidable military force. The Allies, the commentators implied, were embarking on a risky and costly operation. In fact, when General Norman Schwartzkopf launched his land offensive, the Republican Guard broke and ran with the rest of the Iraqi army. But this has not stopped British journalists, and the experts from whom they usually draw their information, from persisting to this day with the designation 'élite' whenever the Iraqi Republican Guard is mentioned in news programmes. To be fair, Saddam Hussein's Guard may be an élite force by Iraqi standards, but the absolute use of the label is a small, but typical, example of the misunderstandings, amounting sometimes to *suggestio falsi*, which arise when concepts are not defined.

Another concept carrying with it associations totally inappropriate to the Iraqi scene was 'public opinion'. Commentators agonized repeatedly about the effect of this or that Allied move on Iraqi or Arab public opinion. But there was not and could not be any such entity in the sense attached to it in the West. Elie, who had devoted his scholarly career to an examination of the reality behind labels, could only marvel that so little had changed since his celebrated argument with his Oxford examiner, Professor H.A.R. Gibb, in 1954. He was then faced with woolly concepts which propped up tendentious arguments. Gibb had insisted that 'the "awakening" of Oriental peoples' and 'the supposed influence of the "people" of this country [Britain]' justified British policy in the Middle East after the First World War. Elie rejected the argument in the absence of convincing evidence, and withdrew his D.Phil. thesis.[1]

I first met Elie Kedourie in the late 1940s in the home of Emile Marmorstein, the Cambridge-trained Arabist for whom I was then working in the listener research department of the BBC Eastern Service. I had newly arrived from Turkey, as Elie had from Baghdad, where Marmorstein had known Sylvia's family when he was headmaster of a distinguished local school. We found we agreed on an argument which was unpopular at the time – in Turkey, in Iraq, but also in Britain – the argument that the Ottoman Empire had merits which had been unjustly denied to it. Elie was a full-time scholar of unmistakable promise. I was trying to combine study for a first degree and then for a Ph.D. at the School of Oriental and African Studies in London with a BBC career. We were both busy and saw little of each other for a few years after our first meeting, although Marmorstein kept me informed of Elie's move as an assistant lecturer to the London School of Economics and his subsequent stand against Gibb at Oxford. I read Elie's first book, *England and the Middle East*, as soon as it appeared in 1956. It helped to form my own views on the modern history of the region in which we were both born. In 1958 we both contributed essays to *The Middle East in Transition*, a collection edited by Walter Laqueur.[2] By then we had established a new personal link through Kenneth Minogue, whose house in Hammersmith I had rented for a couple of months after my marriage, and who was Elie's friend and colleague in the politics department of the LSE. The Minogues were energetic hosts, and Elie, I and our wives often met at their parties and in houses of mutual friends. I had become head of the BBC Turkish Section and my office in Bush House was a stone's throw away from the LSE. Elie used to entertain me in his staff restaurant; I reciprocated in a small Italian restaurant in the Aldwych, where, as I remember it, the food was poor, but the conversation lively. Our meetings were interrupted by Elie's long absences abroad in subsequent years, and became less frequent after my retirement in 1986. But we kept in touch regularly until Elie's death in the United States.

We exchanged offprints of our articles over the years – Elie's stream of studies against my infrequent contributions. We also collaborated. In 1964, when Elie founded *Middle Eastern Studies*, he asked me to review a book on Turkey. This was the first of many review articles which I have contributed to the journal, now edited by his widow. As an editor, Elie was the soul of courtesy and integrity, scrupulous on facts, and always encouraging the expression of well-argued opinions. Outside *Middle Eastern Studies*, we published jointly two or three scripted conversations in *Encounter* – first on the Middle East, then, after my retirement, on editorial standards in the BBC. We did not agree on all points, but we thought along similar lines, not surprisingly since I had found Elie's views congenial from the start. I recognized that they were the fruit of scholarly deliberation for which I had neither the time nor the inclination, and that they were illuminated by an unusual perceptiveness, distinguishing pretence from reality.

Our friendship spanned the years in which the West relinquished, first, direct government and then much of its influence in a large part of the globe.

We had misgivings about the process, and we were both irritated by the self-congratulation which accompanied the abdication of Western responsibility. I remember criticizing Harold Macmillan's policy in Cyprus. 'I see you have rumbled him too,' said Elie, for whom Macmillan's 'wind of change' was another version of the 'awakening of Oriental peoples' – an excuse produced in the West to clothe short-term material considerations with the trappings of virtue. As usual, Elie refused to ascribe change to impersonal forces. He pinned responsibility on politicians and the ideologists in their train, on individuals with a capacity for moral choice. He was riled by the disregard for the consequences of decolonization on the lives of the inhabitants of territories from which the West was withdrawing. He was perceptive enough to see these consequences through the mist of liberal euphoria which decolonization evoked and the *schadenfreude* occasioned by the failure of the Suez operation. As the years went by, the tragedy of Africa, the waste of oil revenues on Middle Eastern wars, and conflicts all over the Third World justified Elie's misgivings. This gave him no satisfaction. He was incapable of the shrug implicit in the remark attributed to General de Gaulle: 'L'Afrique est fichue, l'Algérie avec'. Elie was a passionate, not a cynical Cassandra.

On Turkey, which was, and remains, my main area of interest, I found Elie too pessimistic. He concentrated on Turkey's Islamic, Middle Eastern heritage, while I was more impressed by its links with Europe. I am glad that in one of his last books, *Politics in the Middle East*, his account of the failure of successive constitutional arrangements in Turkey ends with an open verdict. 'Only time ... will show ... if optimism is warranted,' he concluded.[3] Alas, as I am writing this, pessimism is more prevalent.

Elie's distinction lay in his ability to study political ideas without ever losing sight of people – both of the people who originated the ideas and of those who felt their consequences. Throughout his life he was a critic of what he called 'the ideological style of politics', a style which disregards living people for the sake of this or that concept of a radiant future. Unfashionably, his main target was anti-imperialism. He had direct experience of the sad consequences of the destruction of the Ottoman Empire. He turned his scholarly attention to them and to the destruction of the imperial system elsewhere. He was a critic too of the surprising influence exercised by Marxist ideas in Western intellectual circles and of their manifestation in academic politics after the Paris *événements* in May 1968. Although a conservative, and a source of inspiration of the Conservative revival in Britain, he used his pen to decry the inappropriate application of the ideology of the market to academic institutions. His last target was the elevation of 'democracy' to the status of a panacea for all political and social ills. In *Democracy and Arab Political Culture*,[4] he dwelt on the prerequisites of Western democracy: popular sovereignty, popular representation, the secularity of the state. All these ideas were alien to the tradition of Islam. How then could one expect democracy to take root and flourish in countries of Muslim tradition? For Elie, who valued religion as the source of morality, a spur to the acquisition of knowledge, and a proper framework for human lives, 'democracy' could never serve as a universal religion.

It is fashionable today to speak of influential thinkers as gurus. Thinking of Elie, I prefer a term native to our tradition. He was a sage dedicated to wisdom. He lives on, not just in the memory of his friends and students, but in his contribution to the store of wisdom which should regulate the conduct of human affairs.

NOTES

1. Elie Kedourie, *England and the Middle East: The Destruction of the Ottoman Empire 1914–1921* (revised edition, London: Mansell, 1987), p.3.
2. London: Routledge & Kegan Paul, 1958.
3. *Politics in the Middle East* (Oxford University Press, 1992), p.154.
4. Washington Institute for Near East Policy, 1992.

Elie Kedourie: A Personal Memoir

PETER ROBERTS

My attendance at a Memorial Meeting for Elie Kedourie, at the LSE in 1993, brought back a vivid memory of Elie when he gave me lunch at the School in October 1953. He had an air of quiet satisfaction at returning, now on the staff, to the School where he was to become a familiar figure to generations of colleagues and students.[1]

The time of our meeting was 'three or four decades ago', as Elie wrote in *Diamonds into Glass*, when the university had the 'extraordinary power ... to inspire loyalty and affection as the alma mater who bounteously bestows, on all who work to possess them, the prodigious riches contained in the Aladdin's cave of the mind.'

Elie and I had just spent two years at St Antony's College, Oxford, founded in 1950 as a centre of postgraduate research with a bias towards recent history. When he joined in 1951, as one of the first two graduates of British universities to be awarded senior scholarships, there were about twenty graduate students; the numbers rose in his second year. He left on his contemporaries an impression of maturity. This was felt even by the older men, completing research begun elsewhere; some had served long periods in the war. They perhaps detected in Elie an experience of life broader than that of younger members of the College. (School life in war-time Britain could be quite sheltered and peace-time national service hardly less so.) The strong element of French culture in his earlier education ensured that the group of French scholars in the College did not have to make the concessions to Elie they needed to extend to some of us. He then hardly mentioned other aspects of his schooldays but he later gave a glimpse of 'the crude corruption, brutality and ideological rantings which is what the political spectacle disclosed to a schoolboy growing up in Baghdad in the 1930s and 40s'.[2] Writing of the Iraq of the 1930s Elie recalled the *Futuwwa* introduced into schools by the director general of the ministry of education, modelled on the Nazi and Fascist paramilitary youth organizations in Germany and Italy. An official was appointed 'to be a ploughman sowing the seeds of nationalism and of a noble mode of behavior among the Arab youth of Iraq'. He was to be the 'policeman' (*shurti*) of nationalism in schools.[3]

Conditions at St Antony's, rather different from this, favoured conversation. The smallness of the community and relatively common interests encouraged the intimacy and familiarity that go with good talk.

The physical setting of the place brought us together: we lived either in the main building or in nearby flats, provided for married members like Elie. A theme casually introduced in the common room might be taken up informally in one of the flats. People who have enjoyed the hospitality of Elie and Sylvia Kedourie in Hampstead will have a clear idea of the atmosphere in their Oxford flat and of Elie's contributions to conversation. His terse comments brought delight. A pronouncement or autobiography of a public figure would prompt Elie to make a quick character sketch of the author which conveyed more than the politician wished to reveal. A question from Elie often stimulated a line of enquiry which was fresh; others have told me that they realized years later the effect an apparently casual remark by Elie had had on their work and outlook. Lest this should seem too solemn I should also recall the mischievous chuckles which punctuated his talk. It nevertheless expressed the play of a remarkable mind upon not only the immediate happenings of the day but on the major themes of recent history.

His peers and pupils in scholarship know of depths in Elie Kedourie's work which I have only glimpsed. Within the bounds of my more limited interests I should like, however, to say a little about some elements which informed his approach to the contemporary world.

He regarded it from a historian's perspective. He was asked to give an account at Columbia University of the genesis of *In the Anglo-Arab Labyrinth*. The evocative survey ended with the thought that the book might find, he said, a 'modest' place

> among those products of the historian's art – of which Maitland's writings, say, or Joseph Levenson's are a supreme example – that seek to restore, for whoever cares to read them, in all its singularity the meaning of thoughts and actions ... which were once the designs and choices of living men.[4]

The reference to Maitland reflects a determination to bring all the scruples and objectivity of the historian to a contemporary subject. Alan Bullock and Robert Conquest shared such scruples when they were also prompted by encounters with contemporary phenomena to seek to describe and explain them.

There is more of the spirit of Maitland in Elie Kedourie's outlook than that. In his preface to *Canon Law in England* Maitland recalled, 'I gradually discovered that I was slowly coming to results which have not been generally accepted in this country by those whose opinions are the weightiest.' The contrast between accepted assertion and direct observation sharpens with time and investigation but 'starts', as Elie said of history, 'with a sense of puzzlement'. *The Labyrinth* originated, he said, in his puzzlement at the discrepancy between the scene he witnessed as a schoolboy and the picture of the Middle East in Storrs's *Orientations* and the weighty Chatham House version.[5] The initial puzzlement of the gentle and hesitant man gradually developed into the astringent and convincing products of the historian. One scholar described Maitland in terms not inapplicable to Elie's methods and character:

> If he became suspicious of the validity of any piece of received and traditionally accepted learning, he was not content until he had subjected the whole matter to his critical investigation, stating his conclusions, if they differed from those generally held, with an admirable mixture of modesty and courage.[6]

Elie questioned the rhetoric of revolutionaries and nationalists in the same style. It took courage in his early career to challenge it but he was modest when events much later validated his views. In the spring of 1989, I happened to hear his contribution to a series of lectures at Wolfson College, Oxford, on 'Revolution and Counter Revolution'.[7] His talk encapsulated some ideas he had put forward years before. Even then, however, there were many who still accepted that the forces of light brought about revolution and the forces of darkness counter revolution. (A character of Orwell's might have expressed the theory as: Revolution good! Counter Revolution bad!) Elie pointed out much more elegantly that these twin-concepts, far from being universal truths, were barely two centuries old. Before their formulation, a revolution was a political event: the forcible overthrow of a government. The overthrow of the subsequent government would be just such another event. Within months of his talk, more evidence emerged to subvert any surviving grounds for believing that the Soviet revolution had opened a new dawn; few would assert that the revolutions which brought down the political systems in the USSR and eastern Europe were the work of counter-revolutionary demons. Yet Elie was among the first to deny that the breakup of the Soviet Union heralded a new heaven and a new earth. In his introduction, published posthumously, to the fourth edition of *Nationalism* he wrote:

> The disintegration and failure of socialism in the Soviet empire and its satellites has not meant the disappearance of the ideological style of politics – it has produced, in a revulsion against socialist tyranny, a revival or recrudescence of nationalism – that other ideological obsession.[8]

He did not indulge in what people, whom events have proved wrong, denounce as 'triumphalism'. While the former Yugoslavia was breaking up he was specifically asked, in a radio interview in Canada, whether he was tempted to say 'I told you so'. He utterly rejected the implication that he was a prophet. This reaction reflected not only his modesty but his conviction that the historian should not play such a role. Noting that some reviewers of the first edition of *Nationalism* had remarked that he did not attempt to discuss whether nationalists should be conciliated or resisted, he wrote:

> A decision on such an issue is necessarily governed by the particular circumstances of each individual case, and whether its consequences are fortunate or disastrous will depend on the courage, shrewdness and luck of those who have the power to take it. For an academic to offer his advice on these matters is, literally, impertinent: academics are not diviners.[9]

He told his Canadian interviewer, Peter Gzowski, that he hoped the account of nationalism he had given thirty years before was 'adequate' to cover present developments. He explained elsewhere that he looked on the first edition of *Nationalism* 'as an attempt at historical explanation' which by definition was concerned with the past. He admitted in 1992, however, that the 'argument of the book ... meant to be historical in character – has come to acquire an immediate relevance to current events – a relevance which was not intended or imagined when I was writing my lectures in the mid nineteen-fifties.'[10]

The book reflected his capacity significantly to juxtapose events and movements in all continents at different periods: an ability shared by few commentators on the contemporary world. His talk on revolutions at Wolfson drew on Islamic, Hindu and Chinese political thought to demonstrate that the idea of revolution and counter revolution, as inseparable good and bad twins, was conjured up in western Europe for a comparatively short period: it had even less relevance to the interests of millions in the 'third world' when taken up by rhetoricians there.

His understanding can partly be explained by the depth and range of his reading and cultural interests. He simply considered it natural to assume the works of Maitland, a historian of medieval European law, and Levenson, a historian of Chinese political thought, would be familiar to anyone interested in history. We have all been startled by some unexpected reference or insight he offered in fields with which we felt reasonably acquainted. He sent me an offprint of a review touching on the Partition of India when I had been in South Asia for some time. It happened that I had just talked to citizens of India and Pakistan and British army officers who had been involved in Partition. His remarks might have been based on their observations and memories rather than on the sources he had used.

Elie's grasp of events in India and how participants felt about them was not only secured by readings in history and political thought. His interests

and activities were not confined to the study. At the Woodrow Wilson
International Center for Scholars in Washington in 1991, he gave a light-
hearted response, in a lunch time talk, to a request to suggest how Hegel
might have viewed the Middle East today.[11] His speculations revealed his
belief that a political thinker should rightly concern himself with
contemporary events. Journalism was a proper occupation for a philosopher.
He recalled that Hegel was much involved in running a newspaper and
'passionately interested in current politics'. The newspaper was modern
man at morning prayers. I remember Elie's delight when a subscription to
Le Monde extended his daily reading. The immediate comments Elie made
as a journalist were, of course, based on his long-term familiarity with any
subject on which he wrote. This perhaps explains why his journalism stands
up so well to later scrutiny. It also explains why his reactions to current
events were in demand. While I stayed with Elie and Sylvia Kedourie in
New York at the end of the Gulf War, a stream of telephone calls from the
media revealed the weight they gave to his comments, interviews, articles
and knowledge.

Those directly concerned with government also had a high regard for his
knowledge of, and insight into, the contemporary world. He was discreet
and modest about his relations with leading politicians and never discussed
them with me. The interviewer in Canada asked him about his influence on
Pierre Trudeau. Elie made clear the former Prime Minister was never his
student. When pressed about acknowledgement in Trudeau's books, Elie
conceded that 'there were some references'. The open record of
consultations made by political leaders is slight. It is however difficult to
ignore it altogether, after citing Elie's approval of the political thinker's
concern with political events of the day and discussing the two-way links
between his study and the outside world. It may be enough to say that the
teacher of 'government' had opportunities to observe those who governed.
His observations perhaps reinforced his view that the tasks of the academic
and even journalist are different from the craft of making foreign policy.

What is very much on the record is Elie's participation in the public and
domestic debate on education. Like many of the subjects he took up, it was
one which he had opportunities to observe closely. He was concerned about
the direction British education was taking with its talk 'of plans, targets,
selectivity and purposefulness'. Proposals 'for policing ... teaching' did not
reassure him.[12] Such talk reminded him, he said in *Perestroika*, of
'eighteenth century enlightened absolutists from Catherine the Great in
Russia to Pombal in Portugal, with ... their absolute conviction that they ...
were the sole custodians and best judges of their subjects' welfare.'[13] His
involvement in the debate perhaps sprang from his positive regard for the
models of the universities he found when he came to Britain. He described

their spirit with deep affection in the passage quoted at the opening of this paper. It may reflect a conservative outlook but his criticism of the way education was being directed in Britain does not identify him as the advocate of a particular policy of a particular political party.

For it is difficult to place Elie precisely even in the relatively simple world of parties and factions. In more complicated spheres, his mind and character were far too singular for facile categorization. A passage in his earliest book expressed his distrust of the process. He traced the change an idea suffered when it passed from Hogarth to Lawrence: it ceased 'to minister to the pacific needs of enquiry' and became 'instead, a weapon of apologetics, useful for offence and defence'. Elie continued: 'Take the comparison which Hogarth makes between Arab and Turkish government and observe what becomes of it in *Seven Pillars of Wisdom*. Where Hogarth argues, goes forward, then returns, hesitates, contrasts and compares, Lawrence lays down the law, categorical and pressing.'[14] In an article on 'Guilt by Association' in the *Spectator* in 1970, Elie pointed out the absurdities and irrelevancies of attempts to muster thinkers and political personalities and movements in Europe during three centuries into virtuous and wicked squads unequivocally committed to left or right.[15]

It is ironic that instant classifiers have tried to fix crude labels on Elie Kedourie's writings, which defy such treatment. An illustration of such attempts appeared in *The Times Literary Supplement* in 1970. An anonymous reviewer of *The Chatham House Version* stated that Elie Kedourie was a 'Zionist historian' and 'a leading member of the Zionist demolition squad'. Elie replied: 'I am puzzled to know what a Zionist historian is and why the reviewer ... should describe me as one. It would also be of some interest to know who are the members of the Zionist demolition squad ... and what they are engaged in demolishing.' Elie had done no more than, as it were, raise a quizzical eyebrow but it was effective enough for the reviewer to treat it as an elaborate *apologia*. He responded: 'Professor Kedourie now persuades me that the phrase "Zionist historian" as applied to him was careless and I withdraw it.' The reviewer never revealed the name of a single member of the squad to which he had assigned Elie. The whole correspondence may be read in the *TLS*, but it is worth quoting from Elie's final contribution as an example of his attitude to blind assertions:

> I wonder why a simple request for an explanation should persuade [the reviewer] of his mistake, where a large book, I think written without ambiguity, had failed to do so ... he seems to say that ... he called me a Zionist historian and leading member of a Zionist demolition squad because I had criticisms to make of Professor

Toynbee's writings and this put me in the same category as the Zionists with whom he had been occasionally engaged in controversy. This argument cannot possibly survive a cursory examination of my book ... He seems to be so absorbed in the clamorous and futile contests of Zionism and anti-Zionism that he could only classify my book according to his arid categories.[16]

I am quite unqualified to speculate on the effect such a review might have had on scholars and students working in Elie's field. I suspect, however, that more general readers would have missed a rich and stimulating experience if they had been deterred from picking up the actual book.

Anything in these remarks about Elie's life and influence emerges with much greater clarity from his publications. Nothing I can recall, for instance, about the maturity of the young research student can match the testimony of *England and the Middle East*, completed before he took up his first teaching appointment. *The Crossman Confessions* abounds with examples of the kind of pen portraits of public figures which delighted us at St Antony's. His friends, whether scholars or not, were aware of a fundamental preoccupation of the private man: his sympathy for victims of ideological tyranny. It is evident, however, in all his works. The teacher of 'government' was always concerned with the individual subjects of government. Readers, with his books before them, need few other aids (to adapt Elie Kedourie's definition of history quoted above) 'to restore ... in all its singularity the meaning of thoughts and actions' which were the 'designs and choices' of the living man.

NOTES

1. Some commentators have suggested that Elie Kedourie's appointment to the staff of the LSE was consequent to the response of the examiners to his Oxford D.Phil. thesis. Chronology does not bear this out. His introduction to the third edition of *England and the Middle East* (London, 1987) records that he was appointed to the staff of the School in October 1953 (p.7). His oral examination, when he first heard the views of Professor Gibb (as he then was), was on 3 December 1953 (p.1.).
2. Elie Kedourie, 'In the Anglo-Arab Labyrinth: Genesis of a History', in *Islam and the Modern World* (London, 1980), p.300. The article includes Elie Kedourie's recollections of his time at St Antony's.
3. The quotations from Zu'aytar *Yawmiyyat* are cited in Elie Kedourie, 'The Break Between Muslims and Jews in Iraq', in M.R. Cohen and A.L. Udovitch (eds.), *Jews among Arabs: Contacts and Boundaries* (Princeton, 1987), p.31.
4. E. Kedourie, *Islam and the Modern World*, p.313.
5. Ibid., p.300.
6. H.E. Bell, *Maitland* (London, 1965), p.109.
7. E. Kedourie, 'The Third World and the Idea of Revolution', in E.E. Rice (ed.), *Revolution and Counter Revolution* (Oxford, 1991).
8. E. Kedourie, *Nationalism* (Oxford, 1993), p.xvii.

9. Ibid., p.xix.
10. Ibid., p.xvii.
11. Sylvia Kedourie and Helen Kedourie (eds.), *Hegel and Marx: Introductory Lectures* (Oxford, 1995), pp.vii, 192.
12. E. Kedourie, *Perestroika in the Universities* (London, 1989), p.39.
13. Ibid., p.23.
14. *England and the Middle East*, 3rd edition, p.94.
15. 'The History of Ideas and Guilt by Association', reprinted in *The Crossman Confessions* (London and New York, 1984).
16. *Times Literary Supplement* 1970, Nos.3559/62, pp.527, 564, 586, 613. A glance at pp.309–15 of *The Chatham House Version* would dispel any illusions that Elie Kedourie was a Zionist.

The Politics of Elie Kedourie

OLIVER LETWIN

The first thing that I can recollect being told about Elie Kedourie was the fact that upon being asked by the examiners to alter his Ph.D. thesis he had, instead, withdrawn it. At the age when I was told this (perhaps 13 or 14), I had only the haziest idea of what a Ph.D. might be. But I was already all too well acquainted with examinations, and I could savour – possibly with more relish, even, than I can summon up now in the calm harbour of unexamined middle age – the boldness, the terror and the delight of cocking a snook in that way at the examiners.

As I began to grow up, and to experience for myself some of the vicissitudes of a nascent academic career, the full meaning of Elie's act became evident to me – the extent to which, for a scholar with a determination to spend his life as a university teacher, it represented a triumph of integrity over expediency. By then it was no surprise. Although I saw Elie on numerous occasions, and talked to him at some length, I cannot say that I ever came to know him intimately – the disparity of age and distinction, allied to his intense privacy, prevented that: but even across those distances there came, from all his utterances, and from the way that he conducted himself, the unmistakable signs of that same integrity, the massive and yet wholly unassuming self-assurance that arises, and can arise, only out of a long habit of saying nothing but what one considers to be the truth.

Elie was a learned man; speaking three languages, he read deeply, continuously and widely. Trained as an historian – and acknowledged by his peers as a fine historian – he was, unusually for someone with such a training and avocation, entirely at home in the world of ideas. His lectures on Hegel and Marx (which, in reality, traverse a wider terrain) are a classic of philosophical exegesis that could have been written only by someone with a mind, as his was, alive to the meaning of the abstract.

Deep learning, unshakeable integrity, a keen sense of the abstract: these may sound like serious and weighty attributes. And, of course, Elie – with his professorships and fellowships and academic honours – was universally acknowledged to be a serious and weighty figure. But such an acknowledgement misses the tone, both of his work and of his conversation. Never far from the surface, there is in the work (and there was in the conversation) a sense of the ironic, the absurd – the comic, which lends lightness and charm to what might otherwise have been worthy but tedious.

In his essay, 'Diversity in Freedom', Elie took up the argument of Professor Plant that wealth and power are 'positional goods' whose value depends upon how much one has of them compared to other people. Elie's reply was characteristic of his entire conversational tone: 'The enforcement of equality, hopeless as it is, requires constant and detailed intervention, even in the most private affairs. For instance, if anyone enjoyed a great positional good, it was Nell Gwyn. What will the State, what will Professor Plant do about it?' The point is, of course, deadly serious. But it is a point at the end of a rapier of humour, and one belonging to a duellist of great dexterity. The effect, again typical of Elie, is to make one stop, consider the allusion, smile and (at last) see the force of the argument.

Elie was, during the years that I knew him – and, indeed, for most of his academic life, a professor at the London School of Economics. He was part of a circle of scholars and thinkers, under the aegis of Michael Oakeshott, who are coming to be known as the 'London Conservative Realists'. This, to my mind, represents something of a misnomer – a better description would be 'Conservative Sceptics', since the guiding principle behind the conservatism of this circle has been what Oakeshott himself called an 'unwavering scepticism', an inherent tendency to suspect doctrines and ideologies, a recognition of the fundamental conditionality – the dependence upon convention and tradition – of human life and thought. The similarity of this outlook to that of Wittgenstein – though strong, and now increasingly beginning to be understood – was during the post-war years obscured by differences of style and language, leading to an artificial and unfortunate separation of the Conservative Sceptics from the mainstream of modern analytic philosophy. As a result, to the disadvantage both of analytic philosophy and the circle itself, its members were effectively marooned on the desert island of all places the *Politics* department of the London School of Economics.

From this exotic location, fortified only by occasional correspondence with the scholarly world of Cambridge and regular immersion in the intellectual life of the capital, they conducted a persistently subversive campaign against the prevailing orthodoxies of the age – Rationalism, Nationalism, Marxism, Feminism, Collectivism, Liberalism, Fundamentalism. Perhaps, partly by virtue of their *locus operandi*, but partly also as a result of training and inclination, they felt it proper to bring to their (essentially philosophical) task a formidable array of other and more nearly 'empirical' disciplines: history, sociology, economics and literary criticism amongst them. By origin cosmopolitan, and by temperament travellers across times and places, they included within their purview – far more than is allowed, or at any rate encouraged, in mainstream Anglo-

Saxon departments of philosophy – the works and thoughts of differing countries, cultures and religions.

It was largely within this circle that Elie lived his intellectual life. His particular contributions to the programme of subversion were in part historical, in part directly philosophical, Elie was too prolific to mention all his books. Amongst his major works were *The Chatham House Version and Other Essays*, a devastating attack on the Arab inclinations of the British foreign affairs establishment; the *Lectures on Hegel and Marx*; a definitive study of *Nationalism*; and a monograph on *Democracy and Arab Political Culture*, illustrating the fundamentally alien nature of Western liberal democracy for Arab states and what were, in his view, the repeated and inevitable failures of Arab attempts at constitutionalism.

It is probably the study *Nationalism* that best illustrates both his role as a Conservative Sceptic and his own – in the proper sense, peculiar – methods. Ostensibly, the work is historical in character, chronicling the intellectual and practical origins of nationalism and the meanings that it has had over time. And indeed, the scholarship – though lightly worn – is meticulous, the breadth of historical reference vast. But the real intention of the book, as Elie admits in the introduction, is explanatory and, in that sense, philosophical: it is to reveal the abstract nature of nationalism. Elie's thesis is clear: nationalism he identifies not as a deep longing or an opposition to tyranny but an 'ideology', 'a doctrine', which holds the fuzzily and racially defined nation to be the obvious and obviously proper unit of government; and this, Elie argues, is a doctrine without the slightest foundation – there being neither historical evidence that men are best governed in national, as opposed (for example) to imperial, princely, or city-bound units, nor the least shred of a theoretical justification for such an hypothesis in the absence of empirical, historical evidence. Elie's purpose here, typically, goes beyond the particular to the general: the debunking of nationalism – important enough in itself for a generation that experienced directly the effects of National Socialism – is also one more pointer towards the general Oakeshottian conclusion that all social arrangements are historically contingent and are incapable of being 'anchored' or justified by an appeal to abstract principles. The *style* of the study is as typical of Elie as is the substance: 'Nationalism,' he writes, 'is a doctrine invented in Europe at the beginning of the nineteenth century. It pretends to supply a criterion for the determination of the unit of population proper to enjoy a government exclusively its own ... Briefly, the doctrine holds that humanity is naturally divided into nations ... and that the only legitimate type of government is national self-government. Not the least triumph of this doctrine is that such propositions have become accepted and are thought to be self-evident.' The prose there is spare, elegant, poised.

The book as a whole is short. There are few footnotes. There is no jargon. In contrast, alas, to much modern philosophizing, the thing is meant to be read, not merely studied – to be accessible to an educated layman. But there are no populist concessions or condescensions, no coining of phrases, no attempt to make the text suitable for use in an American undergraduate class. It is an example of the English essay in its classical form.

These, then, were the superficial characteristics of Elie's style and approach – a mixing of the historical with the philosophical, a use of the particular to illustrate the general, a learning lightly worn and made accessible to the educated reader. But there is more to say. Beneath the superficial characterization, there is a power of analysis and a subtlety of conception which raises Elie's work from being merely elegant to being important. These qualities are perhaps most concentratedly illustrated in the brief essay 'Diversity in Freedom' which appeared in the *Times Literary Supplement* in 1992. The topic of the essay, the origins and nature of British Conservatism, is one that has received much attention over many years. Much of what has been written on the subject is painful, much banal, some interesting but unsatisfactory. It is, in short, a difficult topic, requiring exactly that blend of historical and philosophical acumen which Elie so completely exhibited.

Elie begins by taking on Ted Honderich's thesis that 'Conservatives ... are simply selfish ... that and nothing else'. This clear, but crude, thesis he rebuts in characteristically pugnacious style:

> This venerable position [the sarcasm of Elie's 'venerable' is unmistakable] brings us up short. We remember [Elie's point is, of course, that Honderich does *not* remember] that the selfish Peel and the selfish Disraeli stood respectively for repealing and for maintaining the Corn Law; that the selfish Balfour was for Free Trade, while the selfish Joseph Chamberlain championed Protection; that Joseph's selfish son, Neville, thought Hitler could be conciliated ... while the selfish Churchill thought Hitler unappeasable. Selfishness will not account for their great differences in policy. Selfishness is not enough.

That final flourish 'selfishness is not enough', with the ironical echo of Edith Cavell's 'patriotism is not enough', has the same comic quality as the reference to Nell Gwyn.

But, like that reference, it summarizes a deadly serious point, and yet a point which contains a subtle acknowledgement to accompany the rebuttal. Elie is not denying that British Conservatism has included an element of selfishness; he is arguing merely that – as his cases (if they do not prove) at least hint – selfishness is not *enough* to explain the phenomenon. British

Conservatism, he is saying, may have been selfish, but not selfish 'and nothing else'.

The next stage in Elie's argument is to offer a characterization of the *form* of the answer that can be given to the question: 'What is British Conservatism?' This, too, is characteristic of Elie's method: being in the best sense philosophically attuned, he is not inclined to dive into a topic, but is instead alive to questions about the nature of the investigation being conducted. And yet, in this case, his answer returns him squarely from the philosophical to the historical plane – because he concludes that there is no 'conservatism out of which, in neo-Platonic fashion, Conservatives in descending degrees, as it were, emanate' and that on the contrary 'Conservatism is no more than what Conservatives have said and done since they began to make an identity for themselves, and to be aware of it.'

Having postulated that the nature of Conservatism is, in this sense, historical, Elie goes on to examine the historical origins of the modern Party. The chain of politicians referring to themselves as, and referred to by others as, 'conservative', he follows back to Pitt and Burke – and can follow no further. Paradoxically, and Elie characteristically revels in the paradox, Pitt and Burke were members of a particular Whig faction, rather than being what were at that time called Tories; and Elie is thus able to refute the notion that there is any continuity between modern conservatives and the original Tories. Nor does Elie regard this as only an historical amusement; he draws from it the serious philosophical point that British Conservatives, unlike some of their continental counterparts, have never been a royalist party, based – as were the original Tories – on a 'legitimist' theory of the state.

More important still, Elie identifies in the birth of the modern Conservative Party at the time of Pitt and Burke the first of what he regards as a continuing history of dialectical self-definitions. This is, indeed the second step of Elie's argument. British Conservatives, he claims, are not merely an historical *phenomenon*; their *intellectual* position is also defined by their *opposition* to certain views held and propounded by others during the course of British history. In other words, Elie claims that British Conservatives have discovered who and what they are by finding out what they are *not*.

The first such act of self-definition Elie locates in Burke's famous horror at the 'armed doctrine' of the French Revolution: Conservatives in Britain first discovered themselves when they discovered their own distaste for a revolutionary politics which, on the grounds of theory, advocated the abrupt and total demolition of the established order of things. Following this preliminary self-definition, Elie locates two great oppositions that have, to date, further defined the Party. There is the opposition to nineteenth-century Liberalism and its successor, Existentialism, the conception that in Elie's words, 'the body politic is made up of individuals each of whom is ... a discrete, absolutely separate entity', a conception which, in Elie's view, is ultimately 'anarchic, antinomian and nihilistic, since it involves the rejection and destruction of all institutions, customs and traditions without which human life becomes impossible'. Finally, there is the opposition to twentieth-century Egalitarians in all their forms – those who attack individual property in the name of equality, whose 'ideal is a level field' and for whom 'the duty of government is to make the field level ... to compel "social altruism" through the exercise of "government with a heavy hand"'.

Here, then, is Elie's explanation of British Conservatism – a party historically born, defined by its opposition to doctrinaire or rationalist politics in general and, in particular, by the dislike of revolution, of atomistic liberalism, and of state-enforced egalitarianism; a party which – in contrast to many parties of the European right – is held together neither by monarchist theories of legitimacy, nor by attachment to a particular religion, nor by a theory of the ideal State, but by its generalized preference for the maintenance of institutions within which individuals can peaceably conduct their lives; a party whose ultimate ambition is in Elie's own words, 'to keep a society peaceable and orderly, while allowing it the fullest scope for initiative, inventiveness and enterprise'.

This thesis has the inestimable merit of being, in the fullest sense, true. It is the right *kind* of thesis, and it is the right *thesis*. Independently of whether one adores or despises British Conservatism, the thing one adores or despises, is the very thing – both historical and abstractly – that Elie identifies. It is because, and only because, Elie was able to move with such sure-footedness from abstract to concrete and back again, that he was able – unlike so many historians and so many theoreticians before him – accurately and subtly to pinpoint the nature of this elusive entity. And all this, in a mere 7,000 words, with a touch so light that an educated reader whose children are not too troublesome can read the whole with enjoyment over a Sunday breakfast. It is an achievement – both of substance and of style – infrequently matched in the English language.

He was a remarkable man – far more remarkable than the world, or he himself acknowledged in his lifetime. As the star of Oakeshott and of the London Conservative Sceptics continues the ascent that it has already begun, the reputation of Elie Kedourie will ascend with it.

The Debt of a Student of Nationalism

PASCHALIS M. KITROMILIDES

I first met Elie Kedourie, thanks to the kindness of Peter Loizos, in June 1974. I had just passed my Ph.D. general exams at Harvard on 29 May of that year and I was travelling in Britain visiting friends and thinking about the topic of my doctoral dissertation, upon which I expected to start work after returning the following September to Cambridge, Massachusetts. Peter Loizos had completed the manuscript of his book *The Greek Gift* and took the time to read my Wesleyan University honours thesis, which dealt with electoral politics and partisan alignments in the Cyprus republic.[1] In that work, my first major research project, I had reached, through the prism of contemporary domestic politics, an appreciation of the force of nationalism in determining normative discourse and in defining the perimeters of political legitimacy in Cyprus. Peter noted this and in our discussions suggested that I might be well advised, since I was developing an interest in nationalism, to see Elie Kedourie and try some of my ideas with him. He arranged an appointment and I went to visit Elie Kedourie at his LSE office.

Sitting behind his desk, Kedourie saw me in a room where we were surrounded by books. He did not say much but listened to what I had to say. He was a reticent and withdrawn man, who did not give away his feelings or judgement. He did concur, however, with the interest I expressed in writing about the political ideas of the Greek Enlightenment with the objective to trace the intellectual origins of Greek nationalism. Just four years earlier Kedourie had published his anthology of nationalist literature from Asia and Africa, in which he had included an English translation of Adamantios Korais's *Mémoire sur l'état actuel de la civilisation dans la Grèce*, as the earliest literary example of the world-wide process of the transmission of secular Western ideas into non-Western contexts. This process of transfer and reception of ideas Kedourie connected with the inception of nationalist thinking in such environments. The precosity of the Greek case, of which Korais was the most articulate representative, made it, in Kedourie's judgement, especially significant.[2]

I was impressed with Kedourie's familiarity with what, from the angle of my American academic training, appeared a very specialized, even esoteric subject. Yet I was thinking to devote my dissertation to it and Kedourie encouraged me to do so, stressing the importance of the Greek case for the understanding of a phenomenon that took up world-wide proportions later on. What was needed in Western scholarship, Kedourie suggested, was a fuller and deeper familiarity with the intellectual background of Korais's political thought and of the process that led up to the formulation of his own ideas. In other words what he suggested I might do was a study of Greek political thought in the last century of Ottoman rule in order to place the emergence of Greek liberal nationalism in its literary and cultural context. This, in fact, was what I ended up doing in my doctoral thesis – when I eventually got around to writing it, which as it turned out later that ominous summer of 1974, was not going to be as soon as I had planned it to be when I discussed my ideas with Elie Kedourie. At the end of our meeting we spoke about Cyprus and Kedourie asked me to review for *Middle Eastern Studies* Tom Ehrlich's book on the Cyprus Question in international law, which had just appeared earlier that year.[3]

After our meeting I went to the Economist Bookshop and bought Kedourie's *Nationalism*. Reading it on the train to Paris later that June I at first found its approach unexpected in that it treated nationalism philosophically rather than sociologically or historically. This was how I had been accustomed to think about nationalism, having been trained at Wesleyan and Harvard as a political scientist. But gradually as I was getting deeper into Kedourie's book, I found it exhilarating. It supplied me for the first time with a critical framework within which I might fit my own gropings for a critique of nationalism. I found Kedourie's style appealing and his subtle, reserved irony particularly amusing. At a closer reading, one could, nevertheless, easily detect behind Kedourie's scepticism an almost inescapable sense of the tragedy immanent in human affairs.

The intellectual satisfaction I derived from Kedourie's book and from his approach to nationalism can be understood by taking into account the academic background from which I was coming. Nationalism was completely out of fashion as a field of study and research in America in the early 1970s. Other things 'were in' in the social sciences. In political science 'political economy' and structural approaches were on the ascendant and political theory was already feeling the impact of the debates generated by John Rawls' *Theory of Justice*. The study of nationalism at Harvard, after the retirement of Rupert Emerson, was associated with Karl Deutsch, at the time past his prime, and in any case identified with an extreme behaviourist approach. I do not mean to be unfair to Deutsch. He was a humanist, a man of great culture and great intelligence, a genuine heir to the intellectual traditions of continental Europe. He had spent all this intellectual strength, however, on an obsessive pursuit of 'operationalization' of social variables, seeking to make the social sciences 'scientific'. In attempting to 'operationalize' nationalism, nevertheless, he

lost most of what was intellectually interesting and theoretically
controversial on the way. In the end, to me at least, his writings on
nationalism appeared a great deal less interesting than what was considered
the earlier and dated literature on the subject, Carlton Hayes, Hans Kohn,
Friedrich Meinecke. As a consequence I never took a course with Deutsch
and I learnt most of what I knew about nationalism from Stanley
Hoffmann's courses on political thought and political traditions in
nineteenth- and twentieth-century France – one of the greatest intellectual
experiences I had at Harvard.

Such was the background I brought to my reading of Kedourie's work
on nationalism. Although not completely innocent of the subject, I was
nevertheless groping for a critical perspective on what I felt, perhaps more
intuitively than cerebrally at the time, to be a profoundly disturbing and
destructive force. It turned out that later that summer I found out exactly
how destructive a force nationalism, especially cheap chauvinistic rhetoric,
could be. After my journey in Britain and France, I returned to Cyprus
around the tenth of July. Ominous signs of a coming crisis were in the air.
Archbishop Makarios's letter to the figurehead of the Greek military regime
whereby the Cypriot President demanded the recall of Greek military
officers from Cyprus, had just been made public. The response was the
military coup of 15 July 1974 which, amidst a frenzy of nationalist violence,
sought to prepare the union of the island with Greece. This paranoid plan
was pre-empted by Turkish military action, which through the massive
violence of two successive invasions in July and August 1974, in the name
of Turkish nationalist fantasies this time, brought about the partition of
Cyprus. I saw my island being dismembered, with tens of thousands of
refugees, dead, wounded and missing, women and children victims of
terrible atrocities and a whole culture being destroyed. The initial shock
caused by all this was followed by a sense of mourning and loss and this
motivated my quest to understand the origins of the tragedy. After my return
to Harvard I wrote the 'Dialectic of Intolerance', my first serious study of
the Greek and Turkish nationalist movements and their collision on Cyprus.[4]

Kedourie's work has been, analytically and conceptually, in the
background of everything I did on nationalism ever since. Other, more
recent books have from time to time captivated the latest fashions in the
social sciences and informed the relevant debates. Although I have certainly
learned a lot from such works, especially the books by Benedict Anderson,[5]
Ernest Gellner[6] and A.D. Smith[7] as well as from Hobsbawn's earlier
writings on nationalism in European history,[8] Kedourie's work remained a
paramount inspiration for my own thinking and research.[9] In reflecting
about my work I have often tried to appraise why exactly this has been so
and I think that the answer is connected with two aspects of the work. One

has to do with Kedourie's major accomplishment, as I see it, in the book on *Nationalism*, which was to take the study of nationalism out of a unilinear and rather simplistic intellectual history, where Hans Kohn had left it for instance, and to turn it into a part of social and political philosophy, turn it in fact into a reflection on the human condition: why people in the modern world feel so strongly in identifying with particular nations? Kedourie's answer to this question points to the cognitive and moral preconditions of this component of human identity – therefore he proposes a philosophical type of understanding rather than a political or anthropological one as the case might be if the sense of national identity were connected with the power of the state or some kind of primordialism. That he himself had intended his project to be philosophical rather than political or historical – *prime facie* paradoxically so since the rest of his work is primarily concerned with political history – is made clear by one characteristic fact: among the issues raised by the criticism of *Nationalism* the only one to which he chose to respond in the 'Afterword' to the revised edition, concerned his interpretation of Kant, whose philosophy of self-determination Kedourie considers the philosophical source of modern nationalism.[10]

I believe it was this philosophical dimension of the book that singled it out in the pertinent professional literature and certainly it was its philosophical reflectiveness that contributed toward its other major aspect, which is its deep, yet restrained and often delightfully understated, critical tenor. Kedourie sets before his reader an interpretative study of nationalism as social philosophy and yet through the lines of his interpretation flows an undercurrent of criticism, which is difficult to miss. Here an Oakeshottian mistrust of the role of the intellectuals becomes transparent, but those who simply detect an expression of 'Oakeshottian conservatism' in this perspective basically miss, I am afraid, the whole point.[11] The misunderstanding of the significance, in a literal sense, of Kedourie's work is nevertheless easily explicable. To appreciate fully the import of the critical outlook set out in *Nationalism* the student of the subject must be aware of the gradual build-up of Kedourie's work toward the climax represented by the book in question. Students of theoretical approaches to nationalism, however, for the most part ignore the broader framework of research and writing which culminated in the book of nationalism. This is left only to specialists of Middle Eastern politics or more precisely to scholars of the history of Britain's failures in the Middle East. Yet without a knowledge of this part of Kedourie's work the criticism enunciated in *Nationalism* cannot be understood.

Nobody can really understand why Kedourie shows that obvious mistrust of nationalism, especially nationalist intellectuals, why he builds such a pessimistic case about the prospects of modernity as it emerges from an Enlightenment view of things, unless one is familiar with his writings on the Middle East. These writings, mostly dating from the 1950s, form the substantive substratum upon which Kedourie was to build the analytical edifice of *Nationalism*. To drive the point home, let me refer very briefly to two political essays of the 1950s which I believe reflect and explain the outlook that was analytically conceptualized in the 1960 book. One is the essay 'Minorities', originally written in 1952. This study of, essentially, the self-destruction of Ottoman Armenians and Iraqi Jews aptly illustrates why its author so much mistrusts nationalist intellectuals and so much despairs of the incompetence of nationalist political leadership. It is this study of political blindness, self-seeking fanaticism and passion cheapened by the lust for power and the greed of its exponents, which shows nationalism at its most sinister.[12]

The fundamental contradiction built into nationalism that makes it unacceptable as a philosophical departure for human action is illustrated in the other essay, 'Religion and Politics'. This is a remarkable study of the necessary logic that drove Orthodox Arab Christians to embrace Islam as an integral component of their conversion to nationalism.[13] What this basically shows is the incompatibility between any form of universalism, be it the ecumenicity of Christianity or the universalism of the Enlightenment – that, according to Kedourie himself, originally begot nationalism – and the framework of values and passions associated with nationalism. This is an extremely important text. It helps to show first of all that the Churches, be they in Ireland, Poland or in the Balkans, cease essentially to be Christian institutions once they become agents of nationalism. This insight, I might add, is of critical significance for the understanding of the fate of Christianity not simply in the Middle East but in Eastern and Southeastern Europe as well. It is a critically significant insight for another reason as well. It helps to show how short-sighted, misguided and uninformed has been the Western denunciation of the values and traditions of Orthodox Christianity, which has been blamed for the crimes of nationalism and primordialism in Eastern Europe. Kedourie's analytical distinction between Christian universalism and nationalism would be particularly useful in showing that the accomplice had been not the Orthodox Christian *tradition* of the region in question, but the nationalized churches which had been put into a strait-jacket and subjected to the expediencies of the secular state. For my own work this has been an invaluable insight.[14] The distinction is drawn clearly but it remains unstated in Kedourie's work. The essay on religion and nationalism must be read and pondered upon by Western observers who remain perplexed by the intricacies of East European politics and would have been very instructive especially to the fundamentalist intellectual leadership in East and Southeast European societies, in the unlikely case they wished to understand the precise import of their endless *bavardage*. Elie Kedourie's work is likely to remain an important point of reference for the self-awareness of the study of nationalism. It is a sobering and serious *oeuvre*, which in the future will gain in significance as the study of nationalism settles down from the current commotion of faddish interest into a field of systematic research and theoretical reflection with its own canonized texts. Canonization will liberate the study of nationalism from its dependence on the views and dicta of luminaries in the latest trendy field and will allow it to develop its own internal dynamic of growth, a dynamic that can only consist in the dialogue of theory and research. I for one have little doubt that in this dialogue the work of Elie Kedourie will command the eminence and respect that is due to intellectual courage and honesty.

NOTES

1. Peter Loizos, *The Greek Gift. Politics in a Cypriot Village* (Oxford: Blackwell, 1975), p.286.
2. Elie Kedourie (ed.), *Nationalism in Asia and Africa* (New York and Cleveland: Meridian, 1970), pp.153–88. Cf. esp. the editor's comments ibid., pp.42–8.
3. Thomas Ehrlich, *International Crises and the Role of Law: Cyprus 1958–1967* (London: Oxford University Press, 1974). Cf. *Middle Eastern Studies*, Vol.15, No.1 (January 1979), pp.125–7.
4. 'The Dialectic of Intolerance. Ideological Dimensions of Ethnic Conflict', *Journal of the Hellenic Diaspora*, Vol.6, No.4 (Winter 1979), pp.5–30. Reprinted in my collection *Enlightenment, Nationalism, Orthodoxy* (Aldershot and London: Variorum, 1994), Study No.XII.
5. I have adapted and applied Benedict Anderson's famous phrase in 'Imagined Communities and the Origins of the National Question in the Balkans', *European History Quarterly*, Vol.19 (1989), pp.149–92. Reprinted in *Enlightenment, Nationalism, Orthodoxy*, Study No.XI.
6. Ernest Gellner's early analysis of nationalism in *Thought and Change* (London: Weidenfeld and Nicolson, 1964), pp.147–78, rather than the much more widely known and discussed *Nations and Nationalism* (Oxford: Blackwell, 1983), has been more relevant for my research.
7. In contemporary writing on nationalism A.D. Smith's warning (continuing a line of argument associated also with John Anderson, *Nations before Nationalism* [1982]) that we should not ignore the 'ethnic origins' which provide an essential substratum for the construction of national communities, is a sobering influence and it is very useful as a pointer to serious research in sources and historical precedents.
8. Eric Hobsbawn, *The Age of Revolution* (London: Weidenfeld and Nicolson, 1962), pp.163–77, besides the more recent *Nations and Nationalism since 1780* (Cambridge: Cambridge University Press, 1990).
9. I should in this connection note a paradox: Kedourie's impact on my way of thinking about nationalism has been running parallel with another influence that it is proper to acknowledge: Rudolph Rocker, *Nationalism and Culture* (New York, 1937). The paradox may be only on the surface, but it still exists: Kedourie, the 'Oakeshottian conservative', and Rocker, the internationalist anarchist, are essentially pointing to the same understanding of the character of nationalism.

10. Elie Kedourie, *Nationalism* (Revised Edition, London: Hutchinson, 1985), pp.141–49. Cf. pp.21–34, 52–3 on the treatment of Kant.
11. See most recently David Miller, *On Nationality* (Oxford: Oxford University Press, 1995), pp.31 and 108–9.
12. Elie Kedourie, *The Chatham House Version and Other Middle Eastern Studies* (Hanover and London: University Press of New England, 1984), pp.286–316.
13. Ibid., pp.317–50.
14. I have written on the antinomy between Orthodoxy and Nationalism, in 'Imagined Communities and the Origins of the National Question in the Balkans,' pp.177–85, and expanded on the non-national character of Orthodoxy on 'Balkan Mentality. History Legend, Imagination', *Nations and Nationalism*, Vol.2 (1995), pp.163–91. I might add here that when I submitted my article 'Greek irredentism in Asia Minor and Cyprus' to *Middle Eastern Studies* (published in Vol.26, No.1 [January 1990]) Kedourie noted with special interest a reference (in note 32 of the article) to the work of the Metropolitan of Sardis Maximos, *The Ecumenical Patriarchate in the Orthodox Church* (Thessaloniki, 1976), which discussed from the point of view of Orthodox ecclesiology the incompatibility of Christian doctrine with ethnic and national claims. In a letter to me at that time (dated 11 February 1988) Kedourie requested a copy of the work for his own information.

Elie Kedourie, *politique et moraliste*

ALAIN SILVERA

All historians worth their salt, said Charles Péguy, seem destined by the very nature of their craft to go on repeating themselves for the rest of their lives. The drift of their thinking and the scope of their interests are already implicit in their very first endeavours, which contain the seeds of all that is yet to come. The rest of their work, carried forward by more extensive investigation into an ever broadening range of issues, serves only to clarify and confirm the accuracy of their original insights.

Here Péguy was harking back to that vanishing breed of what the French call their *politiques et moralistes*. Elie Kedourie, the fortuitous by-product of a French education acquired through the Alliance Israélite Universelle in a distant part of the Arab world, can be seen as the heir and exemplar of this tradition. In the only personal aside he ever allowed himself in print, he cast aside his usual reserve to draw attention to the early schooling which, in his words, 'managed to impart to pupils through the medium of a foreign language the ability to think with precision and to express themselves with clarity'. In that same passage he went on to evoke the memory of an exemplary teacher, a certain M. Elie Capon, 'by whom I had the good fortune to be taught... Rigour and clarity of thought, and a spare and elegant style in which to express it: these were the hallmarks of his teaching, and its beneficent influence is always apparent to me whenever I have occasion to put pen to paper.'

What a stroke of luck that a young man of such promise should have found his niche at the London School of Economics, where he first arrived as a student in 1947 in response, of all things, to an advertisement in the columns of *The New Statesman and Nation*, instead of frittering away his energies in the existentialist maelstrom of Parisian intellectualism. As a lecturer, then as Professor of Politics since 1965 at the LSE, where he took over Michael Oakeshott's famous seminar on the history of political thought, as an historian with interests extending well beyond his chosen field, and as a publicist whose dissenting voice never failed to provoke controversy and debate, he adopted the English language as an admirable instrument for exposing humbug and illuminating the truth as he saw it.

All those who have come across Elie's prose must have marvelled at his lucidity of expression. But this talent was deployed not only to create an impressive body of historical writing which ensured his reputation as a leading authority on the modern history and politics of the Middle East. It was also wielded as a vehicle for imparting some moral truth, some basic verity with which to adorn a story or recount a tale. For if Elie Kedourie could be categorized at all, it would have to be, first and foremost, as a moralist who devoted a lifetime of historical scholarship to explain and to judge the springs of human conduct in public affairs. In Kedourie's mind, moral integrity and scholarly rigour were always complementary, a combination that runs right through his work from start to finish. It is already revealed in the calm assurance of his very first book, *England and the Middle East: The Destruction of the Ottoman Empire, 1914–1921*, a study of Britain's failure of nerve during the First World War, first published in 1956 and reprinted without revision in 1987, and recurs with the same poise and confidence in one of the last essays he wrote, 'Politics and the Academy', an even more sweeping condemnation of intellectual betrayal, which was published posthumously in *Commentary* in 1992.

The introduction to the 1987 reprint of *England and the Middle East* sets out to describe the origins of an Oxford D. Phil. thesis that he chose to withdraw rather than modify its conclusions to suit the opinions of his examiner. The examiner, H.A.R. (later Sir Hamilton) Gibb, the Laudian Professor of Arabic at Oxford and the most eminent Arabist of the day, was a pillar of the establishment who held strong views on the underlying reasons for the Arab world's predicament. In the course of the viva Gibb contended that the disastrous condition of the Middle East should be ascribed to a 'crisis of British imperial thinking' during the War and to Britain's subsequent betrayal of the genuine aspirations of the Arabs to achieve nationhood in the years that followed the peace. A young Kedourie, still in his twenties, retorted that all the sources at his disposal showed that such a version of events was at variance with the historical record and was, moreover, plainly tainted by a species of political advocacy especially prevalent in British official and academic circles at the time. This self-incriminating and arid moralism, nourished by a sense of British remorse and misgivings for having somehow let the Arabs down, was to elicit Kedourie's scorn on many a subsequent occasion. It was to be scrupulously dissected in a steady flow of learned articles and reviews, such as 'The Capture of Damascus, 1 October 1918', first published in the inaugural issue of his new journal *Middle Eastern Studies* in 1964, or 'The Surrender of Medina, January 1919' and 'Great Britain and Palestine: the turning point', reprinted in *Islam and the Modern World* (1980), and scrutinized most notably in the title-essay of *The Chatham House Version and other Middle Eastern Studies* (1970), where all the ramifications of Britain's guilt for empire, erected into a principle for the formulation and execution of

British policy in that part of the world, were exposed to such devastating effect.

How fitting that 'Politics and the Academy' should revert to the same theme of intellectual betrayal and the corrupting influence of political commitment, the subject which had first fascinated him in the 1950s. The article is concerned with the curious manner in which *mystique* and *politique* (to borrow yet again from a terminology first coined by Péguy to describe the ravages produced by the Dreyfus Affair and which, by adding the very word 'intellectual' to our political vocabulary, introduced the twentieth-century phenomenon of 'the intellectual in politics') were inextricably intertwined in the modern world. What never ceased to intrigue Kedourie as he observed the world around him was the peculiar and recurrent propensity on the part of modern-day intellectuals to allow themselves to get carried away by romantic idealism to the detriment of the academic enterprise.

Taking Julien Benda's *La Trahison des Clercs* as a suitable text for his purpose, Kedourie introduced a representative cast of characters to demonstrate how, in addition to Gibb and others, such notable academics as Arnold Toynbee and E. G. Browne (of Persian Revolution fame), Louis Massignon and Jacques Berque (two prominent French Orientalists) showed a persistent tendency to debase the integrity of their vocation in favour of political partisanship and a personal yearning for salvation by means of political activism. In an age that inexplicably saw fit to set up a crude and arbitrary division separating Eastern virtue from Western depravity, they were shown to act out of a misguided conviction that it was the moral duty of the historian to take the side of persecuted virtue and worship at the shrine of what Benda called the 'religion of misfortune'. In Kedourie's opinion, this obsession with an all-pervasive doctrine that idolized politics as a form of individual redemption (what Benda called 'the divinization of the political') had the sinister effect of casting a pall – 'earnest, sour, joyless', as he described it with an eye to the conditions that had disrupted his own alma mater in the 1960s – over the dignity of learning and the true meaning of scholarship.

Kedourie had no patience with the facile platitudes of conventional liberal dogma. Nor could he abide the extravagant visions conjured up by revolutionary enthusiasts, whether in politics or within the purlieus of the university. What he found especially reprehensible in his own field of study was the moral fastidiousness, so prevalent among Western observers of the East, that subscribed to the proposition that the mere contemplation of exquisite mosques and beautiful carpets was somehow proof of political virtue. The cast of his mind was made of sterner stuff. It was rooted in a moral pessimism and a robust scepticism that set him at odds with many of

the gullibilities of the modern world – 'le monde qui fait le malin', as Péguy
used to say. It was an attitude that frowned upon visionary politics and
utopian excesses as a threat to the accepted norms and settled values of
civility, that deplored the havoc wrought upon emerging nations by the
newfangled rhetoric of what he dubbed an 'ideological style of politics', and
that rejected the romantic illusions aroused by national awakenings and the
politics of liberation because they were so clearly incapable of promoting
the development of free institutions and constitutional liberties.

Romanticism was in fact the fatal flaw in the ideology of revolutionary
nationalism – a doctrine that glorified collective self-worship in the name of
an abstract principle unrelated to people's real needs and interests.
Kedourie's celebrated indictment of nationalism, the subject of his second
major work published in 1960 under that title (reprinted in its fourth edition,
with a foreword by his wife, Sylvia Kedourie), tracked down, both in theory
and practice, the false assumptions and philosophical errors of an ideology
of self-determination conceived by its proponents (although admittedly not
by its propounder, as Ernest Gellner, his *frère ennemi*, was quick to point
out in his own book on nationalism) as a Kantian substitute for religion.
Religion remained at the core of Kedourie's beliefs, not only because he
himself chose to observe its laws and rituals in his private life, but also
because the values it enshrined stood out as the last remaining bulwark still
capable of preserving some semblance of order and decency against the
furies unleashed by xenophobic nationalism and ethnic chauvinism. His
own definition of the relation of politics to civil society was already spelt
out in a passage contained in an early essay entitled 'Religion and Politics,
Arnold Toynbee and Martin Wight' (reprinted in *The Crossman Confessions
and Other Essays*). 'In this world of flesh and blood', Kedourie wrote, 'men
strive to build for themselves refuges with a little light and warmth where
they may, with some tranquillity, enjoy their powers and exercise their
energies and their inventiveness. These havens of light and warmth are the
religions that men have followed, religions which may not be cavalierly
divorced from their specific rituals, laws and modes of worship; they are
polities and states which confer protection and secure liberties.'

The same serenity shaped his views on history and explains his disdain
for all the weighty assertions of the social sciences and the uncritical
acceptance of the trendy slogans proclaimed by the new historicism. For
Kedourie, Clio remained, as she had always been, an ironic muse always
striving to grasp an elusive past, but only with the tact and discretion of
Minerva, the goddess of prudence and wisdom. The kind of history he
taught and practised was inspired by the pragmatic conviction that history
could only deal with the play of the contingent and the unforeseen: with all
the ambiguities of free choice and individual activity as revealed in the full

light of plain empirical reality, and not with such abstractions as 'process' and 'development', or as part of some cosmic pattern subsumed under the rigid structure of the *longue durée*, so that all the pretensions of quanto-history, psychohistory, cliometry, *histoire sérielle*, and all their various permutations, were rejected out of hand as untenable propositions because they all rested on a contradiction in terms. To subscribe to any such determinism was for him an abdication of human freedom and personal responsibility, reducing the historical enterprise to nothing more than a stale and pointless recital of inevitabilities.

As he surveyed the claims put forward by a formidable legion of reductionist sociologies of knowledge, he could find no compelling reason, to adapt the title of one of his *Times Literary Supplement* essays on the impact of the French school of *Annales*, to exchange any of these 'new histories for old', since the old ones, sanctified by custom and the wisdom of the ages, had proved their value from time out of mind. History, he declared, was ultimately a question of individual decision and imaginative sympathy, a matter not of science, but of prudence. For he firmly believed that 'in history *expliquer* is *expliciter* is *raconter*; that history has no depths to be plumbed or main lines to be traced out; that it does not reveal what lies "behind" what has taken place; that therefore there is no tenable distinction to be made between *événementielle* and *non-événementielle*; [and] that, finally, history does not need explanatory principles'.

He himself belonged to an older and more venerable tradition, the Old Testament tradition which perceived history as the enfolding of a cautionary tale to be reconstructed from the 'heap of materials' made available to the diligent historian in search of arriving at the truth, The only duty of the historian was to stick to the evidence and nothing but the evidence. In a letter to the *American Historical Review* written in 1992 in response to some tendentious allegations contained in an authorized biography of T. E. Lawrence, he repeated his conviction that 'historians are duty bound to look at all the evidence whether from Cairo, India or Samarkand'. And on another occasion, in an article entitled 'How not to get a Ph.D.', which first appeared in *Encounter*, he explained that writing his first book had

> if nothing else, schooled me in the logic of historical narrative. In this logic, chronology and detail are of the essence; detail, again, had to fit in with detail and no one detail could stand on its own. The building up of details, on which narrative depends was, I had come to see, impossible unless there was evidence, and unless, moreover, one piece of evidence cohered with another. I had come, therefore, to believe that if an historical narrative was to be demolished, either the evidence on which it relied had to be discredited, or shown to admit of another – and

better – interpretation, or else new evidence brought forward which could change the whole aspect of the question.

God, say the French, is hidden in detail. All that flowed from Kedourie's pen showed the same regard for the sanctity of historical detail carried forward by a style of argument that always proceeded from the concrete and particular to describe the general and universal. Description, not analysis, narrative rather than any abstract reverence for the dizzy heights of method, these remained the guiding principles that gave shape and meaning to a body of historical scholarship that never strayed from the empirical evidence.

In yet another essay tracing the genesis of his second major foray in diplomatic history, he was even more explicit on what should constitute the historian's craft. Here again, in opposition to the fashionable views put forward, on the one hand, by the *Annalistes*, whose strict doctrines placed *l'histoire événementielle* under the tyranny of immutable structures, and on the other, the vaulting ambitions of Marxists and their *Marxisant* disciples who believed that individuals are the mere playthings of vast, impersonal forces, he reverted to his own credo that history was simply a matter of bringing the past to life, not according to preconceived ideas or some esoteric method of analysis, 'but only with words to tell how things were'. History, he often liked to say, is inspired by a sense of puzzlement. The history which a historian undertakes, he wrote, 'is an enquiry. An enquiry is a question, and the historian is an enquirer, an asker of questions.'

The questions Kedourie asked grew out of a curious and enquiring mind and a rare intimacy with all the existing sources. But it also grew out of direct observation and the stimulation afforded by academic companionship, whether at Oxford or among his colleagues at the LSE. Looking back on his apprenticeship at St Antony's, he recalled that

The intellectual life of the junior common room, with its impromptu conversations and its informal discussions, worked on me, in diverse, indirect, unregarded and mysterious ways to elicit new questions concerning my own working, to open up hitherto unsuspected perspectives, and to stimulate a critical scrutiny of evidence, inference and narrative. What took place then is not without analogy to the obscure and silent movements of the mind underlying philosophical and poetic creativity which Valéry evokes in his poem 'Palme':

Ces jours qui te semblent vides
Et perdus pour l'univers
Ont des racines avides
Qui travaillent les déserts.

Kedourie often turned to poetry in order to strike the proper *nuance* or clarify, at one remove, the drift of his thinking. Among his favourite poets were Cavafy and Baudelaire, Mallarmé and Eliot; his favourite poems included Matthew Arnold's 'Dover Beach', as recited in Samuel Barber's setting, and Yeats' 'An Irish Airman foresees his death', which he inexplicably chose to quote in one of the last articles he published. And then, of course, there were the French classics of his youth: Corneille, Racine, Molière and the fables of La Fontaine. His first attempts to come to grips with Middle Eastern history appeared in the form of a couple of articles published in Michael Oakeshott's *Cambridge Journal* in 1951 and 1952 under the pen-name 'Antiochus'. Antiochus, king of a Roman outpost on the edge of the Syrian desert, is the protagonist of Racine's *Bérénice* who utters the famous lines, familiar to every French schoolboy, 'Dans l'Orient désert quel devint mon ennui!' As Kedourie was later to explain in refuting Albert Hourani's admittedly guarded optimism on the present state and future prospects of the Arab world, the melancholy mood made implicit in these lines was meant 'to hint at the feelings which the ruinous condition of the modern Middle East inspired in one', a view which placed him at odds with Hourani and his school.

But Racine was not merely evoked as a literary device to convey, however obliquely, the plight of a region transformed into a political wasteland by the intrusion of the West. It also set the tone to a lifetime of meticulous research and scholarly debate which fleshed out and corroborated the validity of his first impressions. The spread of nationalism and the abdication of British responsibility for empire, two of Kedourie's major contributions to scholarship, were already prefigured in these early efforts. One of them, 'Minorities', perhaps the first thing he ever wrote while still a student at Oxford, remains a seminal essay on the changing conditions of the Ottoman *millets* under the impact of the West. Resting on the ironic proposition that the great revenge of imperialism was nationalism itself, Kedourie argued quite bluntly that the Armenians and Assyrians, the Christians of Lebanon and other non-Muslim communities within the Turkish empire were largely responsible for bringing about their own misfortunes by discarding their traditional ways for the allurements of a rootless doctrine of self-determination along Western lines. The other, a wide-ranging bibliographical piece called 'Anglo-French Rivalry in the Levant', foreshadows Kedourie's abiding interest in the history of diplomacy and international relations, containing the gist of what he was later able to complement and augment in a wide range of writings, such as his contributions to Uriel Dann's *The Great Powers and the Middle East* or his essay on Suez in Keith M. Wilson's *Imperialism and Nationalism in the Middle East.*

Diplomatic history was indeed to become Kedourie's overriding

passion: few historians could match his mastery of the Public Record
Office's depositories, none could equal his skill in relating the shifting
alliances and alignments in the European balance of power to a recurring
and self-perpetuating cycle of instability generated by regional rivalries in
the area. His fascination with documents and public records is yet another
illustration of his conviction that history could only be made intelligible
through a study of the twists and turns of political activity and the concrete
description of day-to-day politics in order to establish the truth of events, a
historical genre nowadays both discredited and despised by his profession,
and not by means of the facile metaphors and *jeux d'esprit* conjured up by
the social sciences, which by themselves could impart little of substance to
historical understanding. Why did this man inspired by such at genuine
philosophical outlook and driven by a relentless devotion to personal
conduct and moral integrity find fulfilment in recording the subtle games of
diplomacy and the intrigues of politicians and statesmen? It was as though
Kedourie meant to show, through his own painstaking exploration of the
public documents and archives, that the most philosophical history
coincided in the end with the plain and unvarnished recital of events.

That is why *In the Anglo-Arab Labyrinth,* subtitled *The McMahon-
Husayn Correspondence and its Interpretations, 1914–1939* and published
as part of the series entitled the 'Cambridge Studies in the History and
Theory of Politics' founded and edited by Maurice Cowling, G.R. Elton and
himself, stands out as the centrepiece of Kedourie's manifold studies on the
Anglo-Arab muddle and may well come to be regarded as his most notable
accomplishment as a scholar. Here was a work of truly classical proportions
resting on the proposition that intellectual history and the history of politics
were in fact complementary disciplines and that the science of extracting
information from the archives went hand-in-hand with the art of fitting in
every scrap of newly-discovered evidence to a critical reassessment of the
historiographical context of the subject.

His own intellectual itinerary had already been mapped out in his book
on *Nationalism*, where he paid tribute to Albert Sorel and A.O. Lovejoy, one
a diplomatic historian and the other a historian of ideas, as his real guides
and mentors 'two great scholars', he said, 'whose works, though they do not
deal with nationalism, have illuminated the subject for me'. Written in the
same spirit, the *Labyrinth* set out to unravel the tangled skein of layer upon
layer of conflicting interpretations that had twisted the meaning of the
McMahon-Husayn correspondence well beyond its original intent to
become the operative ideal of British policy *vis-à-vis* the Arabs, a variation
on a much earlier theme already expounded in his first book, then re-
examined, sifted and synthesized in a flow of articles and monographs
drawing on a wider range of sources and presented with his usual flair for

the importance of narrative. But only now that the Foreign Office files had at last been opened to research could he finally find exact and irrefutable proof to confirming, refine and amplify the accuracy of his original insights.

The *Labyrinth* was conceived and carried out with a heightened awareness that there was no real distinction to be made between contending varieties of history or rival schools of 'methodology', for it was only through a mastery of detail allied with a bold and creative leap of the imagination that the historian could ever aspire to recreate history pure and simple. Or, as he himself put it in a lecture tracing the origins of this, undoubtedly, his favourite book, 'that it would speak not only to the amateurs of Anglo-Arab relations or the students of intellectual history, [but that] it would take its place – a modest one, assuredly – among those products of the historian's art – of which Maitland's writings, say, or Joseph Levenson's, are a supreme example – that seek to restore for whoever cares to read them, in all its singularity the meaning of thoughts and actions now dead and gone which once upon a time were the designs and choices of living men'.

In a lifetime of teaching, research and writing, Elie Kedourie marked out a fascinating and significant stretch of historical territory for himself. His parting thoughts on the subject are summed up in *Politics in the Middle East* and a companion volume, *Democracy and Arab Political Culture*, published in a second edition with a preface by his wife. But it would be a vulgar error to consider Kedourie as a Middle East historian and nothing else, for the paradox of his life was that the trials and tribulations that agitated the Arab world and its encounter with the West were in fact only distantly related to his real interests and sympathies. These remained grounded in a European tradition to which he felt profoundly attached by temperament and the conditions of his upbringing, reinforced by a sensitivity for the relevance of a cluster of ideas he believed were of paramount importance as an antidote to many of the illusions that beset the modern world. Not unlike two other conservative historians, Lewis Namier and Geoffrey Elton, who displayed in their writings a similar devotion for their country of adoption, Kedourie also hoped to repay his debt by devoting his final years to writing a history of British Conservatism. Such an ambition was cut short by his death at the height of his powers following a year in residence at the Woodrow Wilson International Center in Washington. What we have instead is a sparkling collection of essays, articles and reviews, written less in anger than with the austerity of a moralist endowed with a rich historical imagination. The form of the essay had always been Kedourie's *forte*, so that these scattered reflections contain more than a clue to the direction of his thought and the thrust of his argument. Along with such a posthumous work as his *Hegel and Marx*. Edited by his wife and daughter on the basis of LSE lectures and published after his death in 1995, or the *Crossman Confessions and Other Essays* (1984), they will confirm his status as a political thinker as well as an historian. But what would surely have given him even greater pleasure is that they might also serve to bestow (to cite a phrase from one of his political pamphlets, *Diamonds into Glass*), 'on all those who work to possess them, the prodigious riches contained in the Aladdin's Cave of the mind'.

Elie Kedourie's Philosophical History

ALAN BEATTIE

The corpus of Elie Kedourie's writings is not only large, but remarkably varied. It encompasses detailed historical accounts of events in the modern Middle East, the nature of international relations since the French Revolution, the impact of economic change on poor societies in Asia and Africa, the logic of historical and philosophical inquiry, the relationship between ideas and action, the uses of philology, the ideology of nationalism, the character of British conservatism, and the place of religion in the modern world. This range, each aspect informed by a mastery of literature in many languages, would be sufficient to establish Kedourie as a scholar of rare quality. Kedourie, however, was not merely immensely learned, nor merely a polymath. The corpus has consistency and coherence. No close reading of his works could fail to reveal either the affinities between the individual contributions, or the extent to which, revisited, his first publication intimated almost all of the apparently disparate themes which he was to pursue for the rest of his life

His first book, *England the Middle East: The Destruction of the Ottoman Empire, 1914–1921,* published in 1956, appears, at first encounter, to be simply an historian's close scrutiny of British policy towards the Ottoman Empire during one particular period, and its apparently narrow compass appropriate to the doctoral thesis which it was intended to be. In the light of what was to follow, it is revealed as very much more than a conventional doctoral offering, and the stature and complexity of Kedourie's thought exposed him (then and later) to misunderstandings of what he was about. Ignorance of with what (and with whom) they were dealing may explain (but not condone) the decision of his Oxford examiners to refer the thesis; the folklore of LSE includes of the story of one his undergraduate examiners (Kingsley Smellie) responding to a serious disagreement about the quality of one of his Finals papers with: 'You think that you have examined him. But *he* has examined *you*, and you have failed.'

The combination of coherence and variety in Kedourie's writings, and the nature of the academic community's response to him (particularly in his early academic years), cannot satisfactorily be understood without reference to the character of the British undergraduate education to which he was exposed. He went to the London School of Economics as an undergraduate, and most of the rest of his life was spent at the School. He graduated in the special subject of Government, but this subject occupied, then, only the final year of three years of study for the B.Sc.(Econ). For the first two years, all B.Sc.(Econ) students were required to read History, Government and Economics. This stipulation was based on a view about the fundamentals of an education in the social sciences, and its catholicity was reinforced by the character of the Government Department's teaching within the School's overall arrangements.

Politics at LSE, when Kedourie first encountered it, was seen as a subject rather than a discipline. The subject was the constitutions of states, and it was examined through the disciplines of History and Philosophy. Most teachers in the Government Department taught both 'institutions' and 'theory', and students were required to take examinations in both disciplines. The teaching of Political Institutions had a considerable historical emphasis, and shared with Political Theory an emphasis on the importance of constitutional structure and legal forms. These departmental characteristics had generated serious contributions to both history and political theory: both Harold Laski and Kingsley Smellie (the latter particularly impressed by Kedourie's undergraduate career) had published a great deal in both areas of political studies. It was thus assumed, in this sort of education, that specialization by discipline was inappropriate.

There were, however, disciplines that were either ignored, or only indirectly introduced, or approached in a particular way, in the LSE at that time. Sociology was a major department of the School, available as an option within Kedourie's B.Sc(Econ.), but rendered marginal by the constitutional and legal emphases of Government Department teachers, and by the death, in 1951, of Harold Laski, whose ambiguous Marxist leanings had formed the Department's main connection with sociology. Kedourie was exposed to Laski's teaching in 1950, his final year as an undergraduate and Laski's last year at the School.

The idea of Social *Science* was, in the School in general, increasingly identified, for Kedourie's generation, with Economics. The Economics to which Kedourie was exposed was of a particular kind. It was taught by people (Paish, Plant and Robbins, for example) whose view of their subject was based on its practical contributions rather than its intellectual possibilities as a branch of mathematics, and whose commitment to the advantages of market-based economies was very strong. Robbins' philosophy emphasized the limitations of economics, and, in particular, the extent to which it rested on foundations quite different from those of the natural sciences.

In this milieu, Kedourie's range of disciplinary interests, his conception of politics as concerned with the rule of law and constitutionalism, and his appreciation of the logic and effects of the workings of the market, were developed and encouraged. There were, however, two other aspects of this undergraduate environment which are relevant to his future intellectual development. The first was that the states whose experience interested the Government Department were those of Europe, North America, and the British Commonwealth. There was little interest in the Middle East (or in British policy towards that area), his birthplace and one of his central historical concerns. The second was that the Government Department, then, was mainly composed of people with practical political concerns. Nearly all of his teachers in the Government Department were practising or lapsed Fabians and/or socialists, most of them appointed by Harold Laski. They were imbued with 'liberal' views on nationalism, the adverse effects of market forces, and the viability of egalitarian democracy as a universal panacea.

Michael Oakeshott, who succeeded Laski in 1951 after Kedourie had graduated and left for Oxford, introduced new and radically different ideas into the Department. Oakeshott was sceptical about the possibilities of political action, scornful of the explanatory claims and practical effects of political ideology, dismissive of the idea of a 'science' of politics, concerned to explore the notions of constitutionalism and the rule of law (rather than democracy), and rejected the idea that it was any part of the business of the university to provide advice and guidance to political practitioners. His philosophy of history distinguished sharply between 'the practical past' (a source of 'lessons' for the present) and the 'dead' past (studied for its own sake), the latter alone being the proper concern of academic history. Kedourie had already embraced and (especially through *Britain and the Middle East*) extended these positions; Oakeshott became, successively, colleague and friend. The academic appointments which Oakeshott made (including that of Kedourie himself in 1953), reflected his views about the nature of political studies: his preference was for people either initially educated as historians and/or philosophers, or who came to share (and practice) his views about the distinction between different modes of explanation.

On graduation, Kedourie's intellectual interests took him to Oxford and to St Antony's. The fruits of his doctoral studies, *England and the Middle East*, were published with Oakeshott's assistance. This book contains, we can see in retrospect, all of the themes to which he devoted the rest of his scholarly life.

England and the Middle East is the story of how before, during and after the First World War the Ottoman Empire was dismembered, to be replaced by a *galère* of unstable, arbitrarily despotic states, whose authority was (unsuccessfully) based on nationalist principles. It dealt with the Great Power interests of Britain and France as they responded to the 'sick man of Europe', with the calculations and perceptions of the individual actors (soldiers, statesmen and dreamers) involved in making decisions, and with the Imperial political structures on whom these interests and calculations were visited. *England and the Middle East* was 'high political' history in the sense that it was a narrative study of the provocations and responses of central individual actors, whose actions and reactions were offered as an important part of the process by which the Ottoman Empire collapsed, and by which its successor states were established and were to be legitimized.

The narrative of these actions and decisions referred to the complicated relation between Great Power interests and concern for the welfare of the communities affected; the invention of 'Arab unity' as an aim; the appeal of nationalism as a guiding idea; the character and dispositions of the actors themselves; and the place of these individual actors within the context of their native constitutional structures of authority. But the central aim of Kedourie's historical account was to explain decisions and actions from the standpoint of the knowledge and calculations of the actors themselves: the thesis eschewed any reference to 'the inevitability of national self-determination' or to 'public opinion' in France and Britain as explanations for their decisions. Men do not act on 'what is the case'; they can only act on what they believe to be the case. The 'realities' of the situation help to explain outcomes and to identify mistakes; but these realities are transparent, by hindsight, only to the historian. They cannot therefore explain the decisions taken, and the decisions themselves become part (to an extent impossible to predict) of the realities. It was this sort of eschewal of 'the obvious' which led to the thesis being referred. Kedourie's position was that, whatever the force of these wider explanations (for which he could find no evidence), they were unnecessary to explain the outcome. He believed that he had sufficiently explained the outcome without recourse to these alleged 'forces'.[1] There was, in the *viva*, no criticism of his use (or translations) of sources; the criticism was based, instead, on his failure to acknowledge the 'inevitabilities' and 'forces' working for the triumph of nationalism. The thesis could not itself contain an extended account of his views on 'inevitability' and 'forces' (this came later); he merely asked that his examiners explain how the invocation of these factors were necessary to his conclusions, what evidence they had for the influence of these factors on the central political actors with whom his thesis was concerned, and why a thesis on history should concern itself with these matters.

He withdrew the thesis. But this experience is important to an understanding of Kedourie's later place in, and reactions to, the academic world. Gibb was a linguist (whose eccentric views on Middle Eastern politics Kedourie was later to analyse), but Joll was an historian, and seemed not to have employed even minimal criteria of historical judgement of evidence to arrive at a verdict. Oakeshott, however, was impressed by Kedourie's thesis, and recommended its publication to Bowes and Bowes.

In 1955 Oakeshott asked him to lecture on nationalism, beginning that extension of *England and the Middle East* into a lifetime's refinement and exploration of its evidence and presuppositions. The lectures were eventually published as *Nationalism* in 1960, a work which virtually created modern British scholarly interest in nationalism. Most of those who later took up Kedourie's themes (including those who disagreed with his interpretation) were colleagues at the school.[2]

Nationalism was an essay in the complicated relationship between ideas and political practice. It took nationalism to be an instance of ideological politics:

> Such a politics is concerned to establish a state of affairs in society and state such that everyone, as they say in old-fashioned novels, will live happily ever after. To do so, the ideologist will, to borrow Plato's analogy in the *Republic*, look upon state and society as a canvas which has to be wiped clean, so that his vision of justice, virtue and happiness can be painted on this *tabula rasa*.[3]

Nationalism was, in origin, a European idea, later exported to the subjects of Middle Eastern, Asian and African empires. The central claim made by *Nationalism*, and reaffirmed in the later *Nationalism in Asia and Africa* (1970), was that nationalism deserved serious consideration as an ideology: it was not merely an instance of 'false consciousness, or of the insincere employment of a manifestly mistaken theory in the service of ordinary political ambition. To the surprise of many, the origins of nationalist doctrine were traced back to Kant rather than Hegel. In *Nationalism*, Kedourie specifically rejected the idea that Hegel was a mentor of totalitarian nationalism (a view central to Karl Popper's *The Open Society and its Enemies*). He continually made clear in his teaching and in the posthumously published *Introductory Lectures on Hegel and Marx* that not only was there nothing in Hegel which could even remotely entail nationalism, but that while the rhetoric and writings of nationalists betrayed Kantian influences, there was, in them, no trace of Hegel. Hegel was concerned with the relationship between the individual and the state (rather than the nation), and his conception of civil society – the institutions and practices which mediated between the individual and the state – had no need for the idea of the nation.

Kant's philosophy was quite different. For Kedourie, Kant's impact on nationalism (and on other influential doctrines) rested on his philosophical individualism. Kant founded moral certainty solely on the internal will of the individual. The natural world ('fact', as interpreted by science) could not generate moral imperatives; and no currently established moral commitments (family, friendship, locality, law, traditions) could survive the test of reason: they were merely contingent. Only the will of the individual remained as a source of the moral imperative: freedom consisted in the continual struggle of this sovereign individual to discover and act upon this internal will.

Kedourie traced the transmutation of this philosophical concept of the person into practices such as nationalist politics through a subtle and complex argument. Kant was a philosopher, and philosophical explanations – theory – cannot logically entail practical conclusions. Such explanations can, however, be adapted and employed by practitioners (Fichte, for example) in particular historical contexts. Nationalism arose from an attempt to escape the awful loneliness of the Kantian individual by inventing the comforting identity of 'the nation'. Invention was necessary because of Kant's teaching that all existing, historically established social identities were unsatisfactory; and the need for such a comforting identity was particularly acute for rootless, half-educated intellectuals subject to the strains (and appeals) of autocracies such as Prussia. The paradox of nationalism was that Kant's celebration of the untrammelled individual will had resulted in the submission of the individual to the holistic demands of 'the nation': 'freedom' consisted in submission and sacrifice to the 'organic' whole.

Kedourie's point, then, was not that Kantian individualism entailed nationalism, but that without its dismissal of all existing communal ties and its emphasis on a continual struggle to invent the individual person, the emergence of nationalist doctrines would have been impossible. The reception and attraction of such a philosophy was shaped by the contingent circumstances of its adherents: for nationalists, Kant was a necessary but not sufficient condition of their ideology. Kant's emphasis on freedom as the manifestation of the autonomy and authenticity of the individual will became transmuted into a doctrine under which all current political arrangements were to be judged by this sovereign and omniscient individual will, without reference to established traditions. Membership of a nation, and the transformation of this nation into an independent state, became the only true form of freedom. Nationalism was, thus, a doctrine which called into question almost all existing state boundaries and established patterns of political authority.

The process by which Kant's substitution of the untrammelled sovereign individual will for hitherto established ways of characterizing personal obligations and ways of life led to nationalist doctrine was, necessarily, the theme of *Nationalism*. But Kant's individualism could result in different doctrines, one of which was crucial to Kedourie's interpretation of the experience of constitutional states – states in which the doctrine of nationalism played only a minor part (if any). This crucial doctrine was liberalism.

Liberalism took Kant's untrammelled individual seriously, to the extent that it found no need to assuage individual isolation by seeking absorption in the nation. Instead, it employed individualism to create an ideology in which the individual could so dissociate himself from all established and contingent obligations as to judge existing political arrangements (including those of states) from an impartial, disinterested, rational point of view. This was the doctrine of Mill, and its apotheosis was John Rawls's *A Theory of Justice*. Kedourie is best known for his account of the effects of Kantianism on nationalist doctrine (through *Nationalism*), but his teachings and writings displayed a contempt for (for example Rawlsian) liberalism which confirms that, for him, the baleful effects of Kantian individualism on the politics of constitutional states were equally important. Both the nationalist and liberal employments of Kant are, to Kedourie, equally important, and his treatment of both strands has been more or less equally influential on modern scholarship.[5] The following discussion deals first with Kedourie's treatment of nationalist politics, then with his views about the experience of constitutional states.

Taking nationalism seriously as an idea involved Kedourie in making the claim that 'economism' could not explain the spread of nationalist practices 'Economism' embraced such ideas as that nationalism appealed to poor subject peoples exploited by colonialism, or that nationalism was 'functionally' necessary to 'modernization'. Kedourie's objection to these explanations was partly empirical. He held that imperial rule was not merely a form of economic exploitation; it involved (*inter alia*, and to varying degrees) great power strategic rivalry, and political and bureaucratic issues of governance. And if exploitation was identified with the market economy, then one had to explain why defenders of the market (such as Adam Smith) had seen the mercantilism of empires as an obstacle to, rather than a condition of, its successful working.

The social upheavals which the spread of market forces and industrialization created were not confined to (or even at their greatest in) empires; Britain itself was the obvious example here, and Britain was notoriously devoid of nationalist sentiment. In particular, there was no correlation between the success of nationalist doctrine and the level of economic well-being: nationalism had flourished in both pre-industrial and relatively rich societies ('Auschwitz did not occur because Germans were poor'). None of the nationalist texts which Kedourie selected exhibited a perceived link between nationalism and economic development, a link which, in any case, he thought to be empirically unfounded.

In addition to these empirical objections to 'economistic' explanations, Kedourie also raised philosophical considerations: ideas were not merely 'superstructural' effects of objective economic conditions. His account of Kant's place in the rise of nationalist ideology is an exemplar of his view of the relationship between theory and practice, but it was widely misunderstood. Kant was not a nationalist, and nationalism is not entailed by Kant's philosophy of freedom; Kedourie explicitly accepted both these arguments. Moreover, he recognized that many of those who invoked nationalist arguments were either ignorant of Kant's existence, and/or unable to furnish a serious philosophical basis for nationalist doctrine. His point was, rather, that a Kantian conception of freedom was a *necessary* condition of the rise of nationalist doctrine: without such metaphysical underpinnings, the doctrine could not have emerged, or been rendered intellectually respectable. Ideas are not 'determined' by economic realities, and ideas are diffused from the level of philosophy to the level of practice by a complicated process the charting of which requires both a knowledge of history (a chronology) and a philosophical appreciation of the logic of ideas. There was, here, none of the elisions and causal crudities characteristic of Popper and Talmon.

Kedourie's objections to economistic explanations of nationalism have often been mistaken for an indifference to the 'sociological' circumstances of its emergence. This is surprising, given the attention in his writings to the intricate symbiosis of theory and practice.[6] In his account, the seed of nationalist doctrine fell, cumulatively, onto social soil whose condition had been partly (but not entirely) shaped by nationalist doctrine itself. The French Revolution (itself a complex mixture of ideas and contingencies), the rise of market society and industrialization, the spread of literacy, the fragility and eventual collapse of the international balance of power, and war, all feature as solvents of traditional family, tribal, social and political affiliations. These radical disruptions of settled ways of life are an essential part of the story of the attractions of nationalism; but they are not a sufficient explanation: why was it nationalism, in particular, that took doctrinal root?

The circumstances in which nationalist doctrines became dominant varied from time to time and from place to place; the point is not that social circumstances are irrelevant to the success of nationalism, but rather that these circumstances are so varied as to defy any but the most simple generalizations. The variety of conditions under which the idea of nationalism triumphed are also important in explaining its eventual development as a political regime. Not the least of Kedourie's concerns as a historian was to spell out the differences between the experience of various subject peoples: between, for example, the governance of the Ottoman and British empires.[7]

This historian's sensitivity to the particularity of circumstance, combined with a philosopher's appreciation of the role of ideas, generated one of Kedourie's major (and most frequently overlooked) contributions to the study of nationalism. Kedourie asked a simple, but previously largely ignored, question: what benefits did nationalism bring, in contrast to its subjects' previous (usually imperial) experience? This comparative perspective tended to be ignored by students of nationalism, because they took for granted a number of things which Kedourie either denied or questioned. These assumptions included: that the triumph of nationalism was inevitable (so that there was no point in judging its merits); that nationalism (as a doctrine) was so trivial or so manifestly false that its undoubted appeal had to be explained on grounds other than its intellectual content; that the situation of imperial subjects was so bad that any change (even to a nationalist regime) must be for the better; that constitutional democracy could (and would) be introduced anywhere (so that even the worst nationalist regimes were potentially corrigible); and that the economic development which only nationalism could bring was a price worth paying for the (admittedly inevitable) loss of peace and liberty involved.

To question these assumptions (at least during Kedourie's scholarly lifetime) was to be self-defined as a 'reactionary'.

II

Kedourie's questioning of current assumptions about the emergences and consequences of nationalism was too subtle to avoid misinterpretation. He 'defended' neither enlightened despotism nor imperial rule. As an historian, he was concerned to investigate the actual experience of imperial subjects, and to compare it with their fate under nationalist rule. He did not believe that European constitutionalism could or should be a universal criterion for judging all governments; on the contrary, he argued that the historical experience of most post-imperial nationalist states made such a criterion entirely inappropriate. The Ottoman Empire (for example) was an 'Oriental Despotism' and, lacking any form of civil society, was incorrigible from the standpoint of constitutionalist reform. However, the very lack of the necessary conditions for constitutionalism in the Ottoman Empire rendered utopian for its nationalist successor states the hope that they would turn out to be non-despotic.

The practice of imperial rule, moreover, could and did provoke resentments which made nationalist doctrine seductive. British rule in India, for example, although the least despotic form of empire, could display racist dispositions entirely at odds with the rule of law principles which were its central justification.

The account in *England and the Middle East* of the situation of the Ottoman Empire before the First World War is detailed and subtle. This empire was the pawn of European great power interests; these powers saw the weakness of the Ottoman Empire as remediable only by either partition between them, or by strengthening the empire through English and French methods of centralization and efficient administration. Partition would generate a potentially fatal conflict between the Great Powers; centralized efficiency would destroy the fragile and reluctantly conceded authority of the Ottoman rulers. This is not a hymn to the virtues of empire; it is a patient and detailed analysis of a tragic dilemma.

Kedourie's treatment of the question of the 'inevitability' of imperial decline was equally subtle. Of the view that the collapse of the Ottoman Empire was 'inevitable', he held that this might be true, but only in the sense that a series of previous contingencies and decisions had produced a situation in which the collapse of the empire was entirely explicable. What he wanted to resist was the idea that this outcome was ordained by 'iron laws' of history, or that it was a result arrived at independently of a collection of past individual human decisions, or that the force of contingent circumstances were such that they could never have permitted the participant actors to have averted the eventual outcome. Kedourie's history found room for the possibility (indeed, the likelihood) of surprise.

Kedourie's surprising (to many) nomination of Kant as the begetter of nationalist doctrine created other misunderstandings. We have seen that Kedourie explicitly excused Kant from personal subscription to nationalist doctrine, and did not subscribe to the view that the Kantian philosophy of freedom entailed nationalist conclusions. But we have also seen that Kedourie took liberalism to be a plausible alternative extension of Kantian individualism, and further misunderstandings were generated by his invocation of the liberal defence of nationalism. He quotes Mill:

> It is, in general, a necessary condition of free institutions that the boundaries of government should coincide in the main with those of nationality ...This is merely saying that the question of government ought to be decided by the governed. One hardly knows what any division of the human race should be free to do, if not to determine

with which of the various-collective bodies of human beings they choose to associate themselves.[8]

The purpose of this quotation is to contrast Mill's (relatively) harmless defence of nationalism with the very different justifications which Kedourie cites elsewhere. Kedourie's point is that such 'liberal' views of nationalism (he includes Woodrow Wilson in the list of the benignly misled) exemplify the constitutionalist's misunderstandings of actual nationalist thought and practice. The latter do not invoke individual welfare or freedom, 'economic growth', equality and so on, as their justifications: 'actually existing' nationalism is anti-individualist, despotic, racist, and violent.

The mistake here is to take Kedourie's use of Mill as accepting the possibility of a harmless version of nationalism. Kedourie's point is that *no* post-imperial nationalisms are based on Mill's arguments. He wants to argue (textually, and therefore empirically) that in the nationalism of the post-imperial regimes in Asia, the Middle East and Africa, the rhetoric and justifications of nationalist regimes are wholly different from those put forward by Mill. Indeed, the sentiments expressed by Mill have nothing to do with nationalism (in Kedourie's sense): they are, rather, based on the liberal conception of the contractual and voluntarist nature of the relationship between the individual and the state. The novelty of Kant-founded nationalist doctrines is, indeed, Kedourie's main concern: for him, there are no 'nations before nationalism', because such a conception (whatever the anthropological evidence about 'ethnically-united communities') lacks the essential nationalist ingredient of linking collective (nationalist) identity with the idea of transforming this identity into its adherents having their own independent state, thus acquiring a licence to slaughter 'foreign' elements within and without their borders.

Kedourie's invocation of Mill has to be read in conjunction with his earlier use of Kant. Mill on nationalism is invoked to demonstrate the absence of any such constitutional/democratic defence in the actually existing nationalisms with which Kedourie is concerned. But Kant's philosophy of freedom (as interpreted by Kedourie) has, in its liberal version, egalitarian, individualistic, anti-traditional, and (therefore) disruptive consequences for *any* state – not just for those founded on nationalist doctrine. Kedourie's views on the impact of the French Revolution (and of all Kant-based ideas) on English politics reflect precisely the same approach to rationalistic individualism as he displayed in his treatment of nationalism: Kantian autonomy (Mill's unconditional freedom of all to choose their own political community) would be disruptive of constitutional states as well as empires. The point is important, because Kedourie's treatment of nationalism became attractive (or at least acceptable) to some anti-nationalist liberals who failed to see that his attack on Kant-inspired individualism and egalitarianism (and on the disruption these ideas caused to established orders) applied equally to their cherished assumptions about democracy and progress. Kedourie himself made no secret of this connection: he wrote frequently on the baleful impact of individualistic egalitarianism on constitutional regimes (especially Britain). Kant filtered down to nationalism in post-imperial societies; in constitutional polities (like Britain) he filtered down to democracy. Kedourie's historical learning kept a sense of proportion between the differential effects of this diffusion on different societies and on different times; but both his critics and admirers often failed to see the consistency with which he pursued the ideas first adumbrated in *England and the Middle East* and *Nationalism.* Kant's legacy was nationalism in post-imperial societies, and democracy in what had previously been constitutional states. Contingently established circumstances shaped the forms of the outcome; but the guiding ideas were also essential.

Kedourie's attention to the detailed context misled many of his later critics. His invocation of Mill as an exemplar of 'liberal nationalism' was designed to reveal the difference between Mill's test of political reform (the welfare of individuals) and the very different justifications actually deployed by modern nationalism (the sacrifice of individual welfare – including life itself – to the demands of an ideology). This contrast was in no way a defence of liberal ideas; while Mill's ideas could not have licensed the horrors of modern nationalist rule, he represented the fatal illusion of Anglo-American liberals that ideas and practices commonplace in their own societies had any relevance to societies with totally different historical experiences. Whether a doctrine of 'liberal nationalism' has merits is not, for Kedourie, in this context, the point. The point is that such a doctrine does not and could not feature in the justification of any actual modern nationalist regime. In the British context, Mill's ideas worked to undermine the tradition of constitutionalism and to replace it with an unstable system of egalitarian democracy. Kedourie's treatment of Mill is thus contextual and relative; Mill's ideas on nationalism (though deluded) are harmless compared to those of say Franz Fanon, but the liberalism on which they are based is harmful and mistaken when deployed in its domestic (British) context.

The ease with which Kedourie's treatment of particular ideas and individuals could be mistaken for approval or disapproval (or even inconsistency of judgement) arises, perhaps, from the form which his writings took. The philosopher William von Leyden said; 'He does not move, step by step, from the beginning to the end, in accordance with an axiomatic plan. He's like a bee; once he's chosen his garden, he moves from flower to flower, extracting all he can from each of them'. Von Leyden said this of Michael Oakeshott; but it is even more appropriate to Kedourie's writings. The same ideas and individuals often appear in different essays, and each essay is concerned with a particular context. Kedourie was, indeed, essentially an essayist; even his book-length writings (notably *England and the Middle East, Nationalism,* and the introduction to *Nationalism in Asia and Africa*) are written as a series of episodes which can be separated out into autochthonous sections. This reflects two aspects of Kedourie's conception of history and philosophy.

The first is that history, for him, was a chronological narrative of the responses and initiatives of central individuals in particular circumstances.[9] Chronology itself provides the structure; only 'analytical history' (of the sort aspired to by the *Annales* School, for which he had great contempt)[10] cannot be written as a series of discrete chronological episodes. For Kedourie, history is not about structures or forces or laws; it is about (and only about) events, and events are particularistic and time-bound.

His writings involve, also, detailed consideration of the circumstances, character and thoughts of particular individuals. This is not 'biography' (in the sense of an attempt to reduce thoughts to upbringing or social location), but rather a desire to specify the circumstances to which individuals were responding, the stock of ideas available to them, the use they made of the stock, and the role of chance (or 'fate') in shaping their positions and responses. These vignettes are thus both an exercise in revealing the relationship between thought and circumstance and a reaffirmation of the difficulty and danger of abstract generalization.

The specificity, chronology and unpredictability on which historical writing was necessarily based arose, for Kedourie, from the impossibility of a science of society: there were no social laws available to explain the past. The point was not that individual action was unconstrained by (for example) social structure, the market, or by the legacies of the past; it was that such constraints were themselves the result of contingent past developments. To describe such constraints as laws was to confuse the certainties· of science (which deals with the natural world) with the unpredictable and almost limitless possibilities of social change.

The emphasis on the importance of the unpredictable interactions between individuals and between individuals and their circumstances was reinforced by his knowledge of the workings of constitutional polities. In such polities, political decisions are made by small groups of politicians interacting in representative institutions, and the fluid possibilities presented by such intimate interaction could not be reduced to law – like explanation. This emphasis on the intimate, interactive nature of representative politics explains his sympathy for (and influence on) those English scholars who came to be identified as 'High Political' historians,[11] whose writings eschewed the use of laws in the explanation of political conduct. It was, after all, this conception of political activity which was central to *Britain and the Middle East*.

The second consequence of Kedourie's manner of exposition follows from the first. It seems difficult to extract his general or 'real' views on the central issues which continually recur in his writings: the nature of politics, the role of the state, the relation between freedom and equality, and between the market economy and political rule, and so forth. Since his reflections on these sorts of issue usually occur (as in the Mill example) in detailed and circumstantial accounts of particular episodes, his readers are often left regretting the fact that he did not collect these scattered reflections into a more systematic account – into something resembling a coherent and consistent 'philosophy of politics'.

But such a general account is precisely what, given his presuppositions, he could not and would not provide. The political practitioners with whom he is mainly concerned do not deal in philosophical ideas. They operate on rules of thumb, interpretations of circumstances, on often half-baked and indirectly-encountered theories (such as Kant's), or take for granted, unreflectingly, most of the practices and ideas established in their own (or other people's) communities. The most interesting of them (such as Lord Salisbury) can be described as intellectuals, but not as philosophers. For philosophy one goes (as Kedourie always did) to Hegel, for example; but Hegel operates at a philosophical level which, Kedourie believed, has no legitimate implications for political practice. Such philosophy can, of course, be used and distorted to further practical political ambitions, but then it ceases to be philosophy. Without Kantian philosophy, nationalism would have been impossible; but that philosophy does not entail nationalism, and nationalists are not philosophers. Kedourie's 'theory of the state' is, largely, Hegel's; but such theories are (in their original form) irrelevant to explaining the practical events with which, as an historian, he was concerned. This question of the relation between theory and practice is, of course, a genuinely philosophical issue; but Kedourie explored it through his teaching of Hegel, not through his historical writings.

There are, however, general dispositions about politics to be found in Kedourie's work. One is that activity is necessarily limited in what it can achieve. Utopian ideologies (such as nationalism) are false and dangerous because they ignore the simplest facts about human conduct. Men are not omniscient; their conflicting interests and ideas are not resolvable by appeals to 'science' or 'fact' (and are therefore simply a part of the human condition); no men (however young) can live their lives entirely free from the unexamined effects of tradition and prejudice; most men seek peace and security rather than glory; and it is simply a category mistake to believe that ideological politics on earth can deliver the salvation involved in religious belief.

He continued to be surprised by the view that the famous criteria expressed at the end of *Nationalism* could be seen as wildly inadequate to the expectations of the modern world: 'The only criterion capable of public defence is whether the new rulers are less corrupt and grasping, or more just and mercitul, or whether there is no change at all, but the corruption, the greed, and the tyranny merely find victims other than those of the departed rulers.'[12] The dispositions reflected in these criteria seemed to him both minimal and more or less obvious, but exploring their philosophical basis was not his objective. He wished, rather, to display them at work in particular contexts and through individual political actors. This is illustrated best in his accounts of British Conservatism.

He had a great admiration for the intellect of Lord Salisbury. Salisbury was (before he became Conservative leader) a defender of the balanced constitution against the claims of democracy. The balanced constitution accommodated the political differences between prescriptively-established interests with a view to arriving at generally acceptable (rather than ideal or true) outcomes. Democracy, by contrast, counted heads and took each head to be of equal worth and weight. Democracy thus ignored both obvious differences in ability and experience, substituted majoritarian demands and wants for a parliamentary process of discussion and accommodation, and turned politics into a perpetual governmental invasion of previously private social spheres. Democracy engendered unreal expectations about possible levels of social welfare, or facilitated redistributions of wealth (in the name of equality) without regard to either overall economic well-being or the predictability previously conferred by a rule of law based on respect for property rights.

Kedourie believed (as Salisbury himself came to believe) that Britain had avoided the worst of these potential consequences only because, there, democracy had been grafted onto existing and surviving constitutionalist practices, and because the Conservative Party succeeded in playing the democratic game so successfully as to enable it to prevent democracy wholly from overturning the balanced constitution – although he became concerned about the extent to which the Conservative Party (especially after 1945) seemed to have forgotten what (in Salisbury's terms) Conservatism was *for*. Of particular attraction to Kedourie was Salisbury's conception of the nature and responsibilities of political decision The burden of decision, Salisbury held, 'depends on the materials for decision that are available and not in the least upon the magnitude of the results which may follow... With the results I have nothing to do.'[13] If the consequences of decisions are largely unpredictable, and if political actors are constrained by a past of which they cannot be wholly aware, what is the scope of political judgement? Kedourie's answer to this informs all his historical writings. It is that responsible actors have to do the best they can with whatever they can make of their situation. To assume, in advance, that some decisions (however unpalatable) are 'inevitable' is both false and an abdication of responsibility; and not to consider seriously 'the materials available for decision' is simply childish. This conception of political judgement lies behind his contempt for political playboys like Richard Crossman, who described part of the momentous process of British withdrawal from Aden and the Gulf in terms which suggested that it was the loss rather than the acquisition of the British Empire which took place 'in a fit of absence of mind':

> When I challenged Roy [Jenkins] the other night he said that £40 million saved in prescription charges is worth £140 anywhere else because of the impression it makes on the bankers ... Well, I've been thinking a lot about this slaughter of the sacred cows and I've come to the conclusion that if we are going to hold the Party together it is essential that we must have some major cuts in defence, i.e. some slaughter of right-wing sacred cows. When I gave Roy dinner at Lockets before Christmas the idea of balance which I sold him was withdrawal from East of Suez and the cancellation of the purchase of F-111 in exchange for two domestic cows.[14]

Another aspect of Salisbury highly congenial to Kedourie was his conception of the relation between religion and politics. For Salisbury, as for Kedourie, religion was a matter of faith and revelation embedded in established rituals: 'God is all-powerful and all-loving – and the world is what it is! How are you going to explain that?'[15] The place of religion, thus conceived, is in the soul and in civil society, not in the political arena. Respecting the separateness of politics and religious faith is both logically imperative and politically necessary; not the least of the harmful effects of nationalist ideology in the Middle East, for Kedourie, was that it had transformed Islam from a religion either indifferent to or contemptuous of politics, into a 'fundamentalist' theocratic totalitarianism which violated both theological tradition and the requirements of political peace.[16]

These views about constitutionalism, political judgement and religion are encountered throughout Kedourie's writings, but they are founded on a complicated and ambiguous mixture of assumptions. In some contexts, the adumbration of conservative/constitutionalist ideas and of the circumstances of nationalist ideology is clearly being offered as a non-judgemental historical account: 'For an academic to offer his advice on this matter is, literally, impertinent: academics are not diviners, and it is only at dusk, as Hegel said, that the owl of Minerva spreads its wing.'[17]

In this mode, constitutionalism and the rule of law are not universal principles against which to judge (and reject) polities based on alternative ideas. These concepts are intelligible only in the historical context in which they happen to have emerged; they are the deposits of unrepeatable experiences (such as feudalism), and it thus makes no sense either to regret their absence or to recommend their adoption, in societies whose experiences are of tribalism (that is, the virtual absence of government) or despotism.[18] English politics is merely what the English have inherited, and the (relative) wisdom of English politicians consists only in recognizing and working with the grain of the situation. The conclusion is stark: it is simply impossible to establish constitutionalism (and therefore democracy) in communities which have no previous experience of it.

On the other hand, Kedourie's writings often betray a different, more censorial, tone. T.E. Lawrence's judgements (as discussed in *England and the Middle East* and by extension in *The Chatham House Version and Other Middle Eastern Studies* [1970]) are ignorant, unfounded and dangerous; and the contempt for the intellect, character and effects of some political actors (nationalists as a whole, English politicians such as Crossman and Halifax) is undisguised.

While the contextual and detailed nature of each of Kedourie's essays is often enough to remind the careful reader that no moral judgements or universal–scientific regularities are being employed, the overall impact is somewhat different. Kedourie implies a distinction between sound political judgement as an objective category (the mere recognition of the realities of the human situation), and moral appraisal. But his tone sometimes conceals this distinction, and the distinction itself is based on a perception of the nature of 'political realities' which is neither tradition-specific nor uncontested. In Kedourie (as in Oakeshott), the view that political traditions can be judged only in their own terms ('from the inside'), turns out to be both an insufficient protection against the temptation to indulge in 'external' moral appraisal and itself founded on universal (and controversial) philosophical presuppositions.

On the other hand, the emphasis on cultural specificity (whatever its difficulties) was, for Kedourie, a healthy working rule for historians. It directs them towards detail and context, avoids anachronism, and protects them against ill-digested social science and philosophy. In his case, it also constituted a powerful empirical weapon against many of his successors in the field of nationalist studies. None of the latter has successfully challenged the historical scholarship underlying his account of the imperial conditions in which nationalism emerged,[19] or responded to his invitation to produce evidence of the existence of an alternative canon of nationalist rhetoric in which the requirements of economic development or justification by a recognizable 'liberalism' played any significant part. Whatever general weaknesses arise from Kedourie's dismissal of 'social science' or from the nature of his philosophical presuppositions, his history has so far been sufficient to confound his critics.

III

With the exception of his postgraduate years at St Antony's, Kedourie spent his academic life in the Government Department of the London School of Economics, from his arrival as an undergraduate in 1947 to his (wholly unexpected) death in June 1992. His intellectual affinities with Michael Oakeshott were the strongest, and Oakeshott's presence was obviously a major attraction of the Department to a scholar who would, as he quickly became established, have been welcome in any major university in the world.

Kedourie's relationship with the Government Department was always amicable but was also, in many ways, distant. He regarded his colleagues with an affectionate, quizzical eye; and some of them did not know quite what to make of him. He had obvious affinities with most of Oakeshott's own intellectual circle and appointees, and great respect for some of those who had been his teachers and later became his colleagues, notably Kingsley Smellie, Reginald Bassett and William and Dorothy Pickles. In many respects, however, the department's appreciation of Kedourie's qualities and interests was not based on any close acquaintance with his writings or identification with his historical concerns: after all, his doctoral thesis was submitted at Oxford, and not at the School. Many of his colleagues took his hostility to nationalism in their stride, having themselves been disappointed by the results of the decolonization which they had earlier enthusiastically supported. But they knew (and cared) little about the Middle East, or even about Asia and Africa. The journal, *Middle Eastern Studies*, which Kedourie and his wife Sylvia G. Haim created in 1964 and edited jointly thereafter, acquired an international prestige which went unrecognized by many of his colleagues in the Department. It seemed remote from their philosophical or Eurocentric concerns, and represented a commitment to serious historical scholarship which some of them neither possessed nor valued. Kedourie's publications (with the important exception of *Nationalism)* consisted largely of detailed historical essays on the experience of non-European polities or on British policy towards them; his philosophical teachings were for the most part transmitted to students and a small number of colleagues through lectures and seminars rather than through publications. Ironically, it was his philosophical colleagues who were most likely to appreciate his academic qualities (and who were most likely to read what he wrote); of the rest, some came to regard him with something approaching the awe reserved for manifestly great men who are, however, engaged in esoteric pursuits. His more Eurocentric colleagues employed their own parochial categories to identify him as conservative, or reactionary, or 'right-wing'. They did not always discern the extent to which his analysis of nationalism was based on views which led also to a radical lack of sympathy with almost all the assumptions of modern European liberal thought. The few (such as William Robson) who realized what he meant, and that he meant what he said, were profoundly shocked.

Kedourie's personal disposition added to these perceptions of him as a great but somehow eccentric presence. He was, for most of his time at the School, the only member of the Department who was by origin neither British, nor American, nor antipodean, and he volunteered little about his earlier circumstances and less about his religious commitments or, indeed, about any part of his private life. Those who knew about his Baghdadi origins sometimes assumed that his (and his family's) experiences at the hands of the Iraqi regime 'explained' his views on nationalism; others (along with the anonymous reviewers of *The Times Literary Supplement*) veered between thinking of him as an Arab apologist or (when an element of reality intruded) a 'Zionist' (despite his frequent inclusion of Zionism in the nationalist canon). That he was a traditional Jew was obvious to all save the utterly inattentive, but this too distinguished him from and to the not insignificant number of departmental colleagues (some of them Jews) for whom jocular, carelessly anti-semitic remarks passed for light conversation (although never when he was present).

Kedourie was first prompted seriously to reflect on Jewish experience when Thames and Hudson asked him to edit and contribute to *The Jewish World*.[20] Maurice Cowling came to see Kedourie's writings as significantly influenced by his religious disposition, although Kedourie himself was surprised at this reading, and it is unclear whether he regarded it as legitimate.[21]

He was alarmingly learned, formidably well informed about topics remote from his specialist concerns, and fluent (from sources which he smilingly always refused to divulge) in even the remoter reaches of idiomatic English.[22] Those who took it upon themselves to impress him with their knowledge of (say) opera, poetry or painting were often disconcerted to discover later (though never from him) that he knew much more than they did.

Kedourie was not an easy colleague for those who liked small talk or superficial clubbability. He knew little and cared less about the private lives of most of his colleagues; he was impatient of gossip about them; he judged them primarily as scholars, and could round with surprising (for him) vehemence on those who allowed social snobbery or racial prejudice to affect their assessment of academic merit. The judgement could appear forbidding, even in informal circumstances. A visiting academic, staying with him, recounted producing at Sunday breakfast a copy of the 'quality' Sunday newspaper which he took. Kedourie read aloud, without comment, the headlines and subheadings in the paper. 'He made them sound', his visitor or recalls, 'either utterly trivial or absurd, and made me feel foolish for concerning myself with them.'

The cryptic comments in which Kedourie, on informal occasions, would encapsulate his views could be startling and appear designed to end rather than to invite debate: 'He was a Whig' (a dismissal of Burke); 'It is a slave plantation' (Nasser's Egypt); 'He is the intellectual counterpart of Madam Blavatsky' (Marx); 'Politicians cannot take decisions with a view to their consequences' (on political judgement). Such remarks were usually accompanied by a seismic shrug, or by the characteristic chuckle which emphasized the degree of his contempt. But even his most provocative epigrams usually turned out to be but the tip of a carefully constructed and massive intellectual iceberg.[23] One sometimes came to appreciate this only years after they were first encountered. An undergraduate who presented him with a banal 'Whiggish' essay on the British Constitution complained that Kedourie had merely remarked: 'Go to the Foreign Office. Look at the buttons on the uniform of the messengers. You will see the Crown on them.' Much later, he came to appreciate the point: that British constitutional practices and ideas reflect a considerable number of non-democratic assumptions, and that this fact is not evidence of 'a democracy which is a noble lie'. Rather, it is evidence of the serious limits of democracy as a concept adequate to describe British political culture. Kedourie was generous with his advice and help to those who asked for it; and those of us who came to feel a great personal affection for him did so in part because of his capacity to be companionable without feeling (or making us feel) the need to chatter.

The felicity of his own family life and his quiet but firm views about proper conduct must have made the sometimes tangled personal lives of others puzzling and distasteful to him; but those he liked and respected were offered quiet and effective support when they needed it. He was an academic who exemplified the Aristotelian virtues: admirable in character, quietly companionable, a friend in need, always the teacher yet blissfully unaware of the onus he imposed when he treated the pupil as simultaneously his intellectual peer. Kedourie's own conception of the teacher was expressed in his tribute to Martin Wight: 'a teacher whose greatest and most seminal influence was in large measure expressed in lectures, tutorials, seminars and discussion groups. Exercised that is by means of the spoken, the living, word transmitted directly person to person, mind to mind.'[24] To most of his students, he himself would not have appeared as a theatrical or spectacular teacher. He lectured from a script, written as if for publication, rather than in the easy, impromptu style adopted by many of his colleagues. He spoke in a low, calm, monotone, with no dramatic gestures, head down to the lectern to read his script, often straining the hearing of his audience. His lectures in the introductory History of Political Thought course (originally taught by Oakeshott) were often regarded as tedious, but to those with sufficient interest and imagination to discount the manner and to interpret them as a teacher reading from a sophisticated and illuminating text they were profound, provocative and instructive.

The content of his lectures on nationalism were particularly impressive. They were lucid, well organized and logically sequential. Some of us discovered Kant through them, others were introduced to nationalist writings for the first time, doubtless sometimes (in Kedourie's view) with adverse consequences. These lectures were not compulsory, but word spread about their quality: note-takers, philosophers, and triflers alike attended. It is unlikely that, when he gave up the lectures on the publication of *Nationalism*, as many students read the book as had learned from the lectures. In his early years as a teacher in the Department, he appeared shy and diffident. Later, as his reputation and self-confidence grew, he could adopt an arrogant and dismissive tone in classes and seminars. He did not suffer fools gladly (although his harshest comments were reserved for academic colleagues rather than students) and his conception of teaching in a university was individual, if not unique. He was uncomfortable with the idea of lectures as substitutes for reading or as imparting (on the model of economics and the natural sciences) a 'basic toolkit' which could be examined by (for example) multiple-choice tests. This was why he ceased to lecture on nationalism on the publication of his book. He was scornful of the deployment of personal computers (and even typewriters) – 'gadgets' – preferring to write the final version in a longhand needing little revision ('I don't start writing until I am entirely clear as to what I'm going to say'). Nor was he entirely at ease in informal seminars where discussion became alternately adversarial, unfocused, or undirected. He was happiest when elucidating texts to a group of colleagues or students (occasions known affectionately as 'Elie's Bible classes'), or assisting graduate students and colleagues with particular problems in the interpretation of sources. He had an unrivalled ability to tease out information from a single document, and to piece together original and coherent accounts or suggestions from a collection of disparate and apparently unrelated sources. He was an unfailingly fecund supervisor, even for graduate students working in fields remote from his own.

As his reputation grew, he regularly took up visiting appointments at universities in North America, France, Israel and Australia. These absences were sometimes resented by some of his younger colleagues. But he was, for most of his academic life, one of the few members of the Department whose scholarly reputation attracted such invitations; he did not conceive of teaching mainly as a matter of fulfilling timetabled lecturing obligations; his scholarly affinities were as much with colleagues outside as inside the School; and developments at the School (as in British universities generally) had made it less congenial to him.

For Kedourie, a university was a library surrounded by scholars who were skilled in the explication of texts and documentary evidence. It was (or should be) concerned only with instilling an appreciation of intellectual enquiry. He was distressed by the extent to which this conception was being replaced by an emphasis on 'relevance' and vocational training, and subject to increasing and detailed governmental regulation. Political studies at the School were increasingly divorced (through specialization) from other disciplines (notably economics and history), and teaching and examining were becoming bureaucratically formalized (from both within and without): universities were ceasing to be a community of self-regulating scholars. Oakeshott had been, for Kedourie, a guarantor of resistance to these developments and of the preservation of an 'Oxbridge' view of academic community; after Oakeshott's retirement, he feared that 'the game is up' (a revealing reference to a favourite anecdote of Oakeshott's about one sort of reaction to the 1870 Education Act). Kedourie did not find it easy to deal with these developments. He disliked internal academic politics as a distraction from his scholarly pursuits, was dismayed by the lack of success he encountered on the few occasions when he was moved to lobby the School authorities, and confined himself to writing (with no great hope of success) elegant appeals to politicians and the academic community.[25] After Oakeshott's retirement, he was subject once again to the spectacle of university colleagues failing to uphold what he saw as the basic conditions of their own institution. As an undergraduate, his merits had not been sufficiently recognized; the submission of his Oxford D.Phil. thesis had been criticized on grounds which he found shockingly irrelevant to historical scholarship. Towards the end of his time at the school, he found himself once again governed by those who did not share his own austere academic standards.

His early death cut short what would have been a continuation of his prolific scholarly activity. There was one project, in particular, towards which he had long been reflecting and (as he put it) 'jotting': an account of the idea of Conservatism. The consolation here is that his published essays leave one in no doubt about his general conception of the course of British Conservative history, and about what he thought of some of its exemplars (such as Salisbury) and some of its less satisfactory mutations (Halifax). What we will never have is an extension of these beautifully painted and discriminating portraits of individual character, disposition and circumstance, so effective in linking the general argument with the particular instance.

A second project – his interpretation of the philosophy of Hegel – was fortunately nearer to fruition, and has been published since his death.[26] This will be some recompense for the most obvious lacuna in the legacy of his published works: an independent and extensive account of his own conception of political philosophy.

NOTES

1. *England and the Middle East* (1987 edition), pp.1–7.
2. They include Ernest Gellner, Anthony Smith, James Mayall, and Brendan O'Leary.
3. *Nationalism*, pp.xiii–xiv. All references to this work are to the fourth edition (1993), unless otherwise indicated.
4. The central characterization of nationalism in Ernest Gellner's *Nations and Nationalism*.
5. Examples include Maurice Cowling, *Mill and Liberalism*, and Kenneth Minogue, *The Liberal Mind* and *Nationalism*.
6. See, for example, Elie Kedourie and Sylvia G. Haim (eds.), *Essays on the Economic History of the Middle East* (1988).
7. *Democracy and Arab Political Culture* (1993).
8. John Stuart Mill, *Considerations on Representative Government*, cited in Kedourie, *Nationalism* (4th ed., p.127).
9. *Arab Political Memoirs and Other Studies* (1974).
10. 'New Histories for Old', in *The Crossman Confessions and Other Essays*, pp.159–76.
11. For an account of this 'school', with references to Kedourie's relationship to it, see M. Cowling, *Religion and Public Doctrine in Modern England*, Vol.1.
12. *Nationalism*, p.135. Ernest Gellner's criticism of the criteria as hopelessly anachronistic appears in his *Nations and Nationalism*.
13. Lord Salisbury, quoted in 'Lord Salisbury and Politics', *The Crossman Confessions and Other Essays* (1984), p.52.
14. R.H.S. Crossman, *Diaries of a Cabinet Minister*: Vol.2, *Lord President of the Council and Leader of the House of Commons, 1966–1968*. Entry for 27 December 1967, quoted in *The Crossman Confessions and Other Essays*, p.21.
15. Lord Salisbury, quoted in 'Lord Salisbury and Politics', op. cit. p.51. See also the reflections on religion in *The Crossman Confessions and Other Essays*.
16. See, *inter alia*, *Afghani and 'Abduh: An Essay on Religious Unbelief and Political Activism in Modern Islam* (1966); *Islam in the Modern World and Other Studies* (1980).
17. *Nationalism* (1961 ed.), Preface.
18. *Democracy and Arab Political Culture* (1993).
19. For his diligence in establishing the robustness of the conclusions of *England and the Middle East*, see *In the Anglo-Arab Labyrinth: The McMahon-Husayn Correspondence and its Interpretations, 1914–1939* (1976).
20. A commission he was initially reluctant to undertake. This paragraph is based on a conversation with Sylvia Haim.

21. In *Religious and Public Doctrine*, op. cit.
22. Some sentences in the next few paragraphs have previously appeared in Alan Beattie, 'Elie Kedourie', in *The Jewish Journal of Sociology*, Autumn 1992.
23. See, for example, E. Kedourie and Sylvia G. Haim (eds.), *Modern Egypt: Studies in Politics and Society* (1980), and idem, *Politics in the Middle East* (1992).
24. 'Religion and Politics: Arnold Toynbee and Martin Wight', in *The Crossman Confessions and Other Essays*, p.207.
25. *Diamonds into Glass: The Government and the Universities* (1988); *Perestroika in the Universities* (1989).
26. Sylvia Kedourie and Helen Kedourie (eds.), *Hegel and Marx: Introductory Lectures* (1995).